T0143820

Ideas of Good and Evil

Ideas of Good and Evil

William Butler Yeats

MINT EDITIONS

Ideas of Good and Evil was first published in 1903.

This edition published by Mint Editions 2020.

ISBN 9781513270883 | E-ISBN 9781513275888

Published by Mint Editions®

 MINT
EDITIONS

minteditionbooks.com

Publishing Director: Jennifer Newens
Design & Production: Rachel Lopez Metzger
Project Manager: Micaela Clark
Typesetting: Westchester Publishing Services

Contents

What is 'Popular Poetry'?

I think it was a Young Ireland Society that set my mind running on 'popular poetry.' We used to discuss everything that was known to us about Ireland, and especially Irish literature and Irish history. We had no Gaelic, but paid great honour to the Irish poets who wrote in English, and quoted them in our speeches. I could have told you at that time the dates of the birth and death, and quoted the chief poems, of men whose names you have not heard, and perhaps of some whose names I have forgotten. I knew in my heart that the most of them wrote badly, and yet such romance clung about them, such a desire for Irish poetry was in all our minds, that I kept on saying, not only to others but to myself, that most of them wrote well, or all but well. I had read Shelley and Spenser and had tried to mix their styles together in a pastoral play which I have not come to dislike much, and yet I do not think Shelley or Spenser ever moved me as did these poets. I thought one day—I can remember the very day when I thought it—'If somebody could make a style which would not be an English style and yet would be musical and full of colour, many others would catch fire from him, and we would have a really great school of ballad poetry in Ireland. If these poets, who have never ceased to fill the newspapers and the ballad-books with their verses, had a good tradition they would write beautifully and move everybody as they move me.' Then a little later on I thought, 'If they had something else to write about besides political opinions, if more of them would write about the beliefs of the people like Allingham, or about old legends like Ferguson, they would find it easier to get a style.' Then, with a deliberateness that still surprises me, for in my heart of hearts I have never been quite certain that one should be more than an artist, that even patriotism is more than an impure desire in an artist, I set to work to find a style and things to write about that the ballad writers might be the better.

They are no better, I think, and my desire to make them so was, it may be, one of the illusions Nature holds before one, because she knows that the gifts she has to give are not worth troubling about. It is for her sake that we must stir ourselves, but we would not trouble to get out of bed in the morning, or to leave our chairs once we are in them, if she had not her conjuring bag. She wanted a few verses from me, and because it would not have seemed worth while taking so much trouble to see my books lie on a few drawing-room tables, she filled my head with thoughts of making a whole literature, and plucked me out of the Dublin art schools where I should have stayed drawing from the round, and sent me into a library to read bad translations from the Irish, and at last down into Connaught to sit by turf fires. I wanted to write 'popular poetry' like those Irish poets, for I believed that all good literatures were popular, and even cherished the fancy that the Adelphi melodrama, which I had never seen, might be good literature, and I hated what I called the coteries. I thought that one must write without care, for that was of the coteries, but with a gusty energy that would put all straight if it came out of the right heart. I had a conviction, which indeed I have still, that one's verses should hold, as in a mirror, the colours of one's own climate and scenery in their right proportion; and, when I found my verses too full of the reds and yellows Shelley gathered in Italy, I thought for two days of setting things right, not as I should now by making my rhythms faint and nervous and filling my images with a certain coldness, a certain wintry wildness, but by eating little and sleeping upon a board. I felt indignant with Matthew Arnold because he complained that somebody, who had translated Homer into a ballad measure, had tried to write epic to the tune of Yankee Doodle. It seemed to me that it did not matter what tune one wrote to, so long as that gusty energy came often enough and strongly enough. And I delighted in Victor Hugo's book upon Shakespeare, because he abused critics and coteries and thought that Shakespeare wrote without care or premeditation and to please everybody. I would indeed have had every illusion had I believed in that straightforward logic, as of newspaper articles, which so tickles the ears of the shopkeepers; but I always knew that the line of Nature is crooked, that, though we dig the canal beds as straight as we can, the rivers run hither and thither in their wildness.

From that day to this I have been busy among the verses and stories that the people make for themselves, but I had been busy a very little while before I knew that what we call popular poetry never came from the people at all. Longfellow, and Campbell, and Mrs. Hemans, and Macaulay in his *Lays*, and Scott in his longer poems are the poets of the middle class, of people who have unlearned the unwritten tradition which binds the unlettered, so long as they are masters of themselves, to the beginning of time and to the foundation of the world, and who have not learned the written tradition which has been established upon the unwritten. I became certain that Burns, whose greatness has been used to justify the littleness of others, was in part a poet of the middle class, because though the farmers he sprang from and lived among had been able to create a little tradition of their own, less a tradition of ideas than of speech, they had been divided by religious and political changes from the images and emotions which had once carried their memories backward thousands of years. Despite his expressive speech which sets him above all other popular poets, he has the triviality of emotion, the poverty of ideas, the imperfect sense of beauty of a poetry whose most typical expression is in Longfellow. Longfellow has his popularity, in the main, because he tells his story or his idea so that one needs nothing but his verses to understand it. No words of his borrow their beauty from those that used them before, and one can get all that there is in story and idea without seeing them, as if moving before a half-faded curtain embroidered with kings and queens, their loves and battles and their days out hunting, or else with holy letters and images of so great antiquity that nobody can tell the god or goddess they would commend to an unfading memory. Poetry that is not popular poetry presupposes, indeed, more than it says, though we, who cannot know what it is to be disinherited, only understand how much more, when we read it in its most typical expressions, in the *Epipsychidion* of Shelley, or in Spenser's description of the gardens of Adonis, or when we meet the misunderstandings of others. Go down into the street and read to your baker or your candlestick-maker any poem which is not popular poetry. I have heard a baker, who was clever enough with his oven, deny that Tennyson could have known what he was writing when he wrote 'Warming his five wits, the white owl in the belfry sits,' and once when I read out Omar Khayyam to one of the best of candlestick-makers, he said, 'What is the meaning of "we come like water and like wind we go"?' Or go down into the street with some thought whose bare meaning must be plain to everybody; take with you Ben Jonson's 'Beauty like sorrow dwelleth everywhere,' and find out how utterly its enchantment depends on an association of beauty with sorrow which written tradition has from the unwritten, which had it in its turn from ancient religion; or take with you these lines in whose bare meaning also there is nothing to stumble over, and find out what men lose who are not in love with Helen.

> *'Brightness falls from the air,*
> *Queens have died young and fair,*
> *Dust hath closed Helen's eye.'*

I pick my examples at random, for I am writing where I have no books to turn the pages of, but one need not go east of the sun or west of the moon in so simple a matter.

On the other hand, when Walt Whitman writes in seeming defiance of tradition, he needs tradition for his protection, for the butcher and the baker and the candlestick-maker grow merry over him when they meet his work by chance. Nature, which cannot endure emptiness, has made them gather conventions which cannot disguise their low birth though they copy, as from far off, the dress and manners of the well-bred and the well-born. The gatherers mock all expression that is wholly unlike their own, just as little boys in the street mock at strangely-dressed people and at old men who talk to themselves.

There is only one kind of good poetry, for the poetry of the coteries, which presupposes the written tradition, does not differ in kind from the true poetry of the people, which presupposes the unwritten tradition. Both are alike strange and obscure, and unreal to all who have not understanding, and both, instead of that manifest logic, that clear rhetoric of the 'popular poetry,' glimmer with thoughts and images whose 'ancestors were stout and wise,' 'anigh to Paradise' 'ere yet men knew the gift of corn.' It may be that we know as little of their descent as men knew of 'the man born to be a king' when they found him in that cradle marked with the red lion crest, and yet we know somewhere in the heart that they have been sung in temples, in ladies' chambers, and our nerves quiver with a recognition they were shaped to by a thousand emotions. If men did not remember or half remember impossible things, and, it may be, if the worship of sun and moon had not left a faint reverence behind it, what Aran fisher-girl would sing—

'It is late last night the dog was speaking of you; the snipe was speaking of you in her deep marsh. It is you are the lonely bird throughout the woods; and that you may be without a mate until you find me.

'You promised me and you said a lie to me, that you would be before me where the sheep are flocked. I gave a whistle and three hundred cries to you; and I found nothing there but a bleating lamb.

'You promised me a thing that was hard for you, a ship of gold under a silver mast; twelve towns and a market in all of them, and a fine white court by the side of the sea.

'You promised me a thing that is not possible; that you would give me gloves of the skin of a fish; that you would give me shoes of the skin of a bird, and a suit of the dearest silk in Ireland.

'My mother said to me not to be talking with you, to-day or to-morrow or on Sunday. It was a bad time she took for telling me that, it was shutting the door after the house was robbed. . .

'You have taken the east from me, you have taken the west from me, you have taken what is before me and what is behind me; you have taken the moon, you have taken the sun from me, and my fear is great you have taken God from me.'

The Gael of the Scottish islands could not sing his beautiful song over a bride, had he not a memory of the belief that Christ was the only man who measured six feet and not a little more or less, and was perfectly shaped in all other ways, and if he did not remember old symbolical observances—

> *I bathe thy palms*
> *In showers of wine,*
> *In the cleansing fire,*
> *In the juice of raspberries,*
> *In the milk of honey.*
>
> * * * * *
>
> *Thou art the joy of all joyous things,*
> *Thou art the light of the beam of the sun,*
> *Thou art the door of the chief of hospitality,*
> *Thou art the surpassing pilot star,*
> *Thou art the step of the deer of the hill,*
> *Thou art the step of the horse of the plain,*
> *Thou art the grace of the sun rising,*
> *Thou art the loveliness of all lovely desires.*
>
> *The lovely likeness of the Lord*
> *Is in thy pure face,*
> *The loveliest likeness that was upon earth.*

I soon learned to cast away one other illusion of 'popular poetry.' I learned from the people themselves, before I learned it from any book, that they cannot separate the idea of an art or a craft from the idea of a cult with ancient technicalities and mysteries. They can hardly separate mere learning from witchcraft, and are fond of words and verses that keep half their secret to themselves. Indeed, it is certain that before the counting-house had created a new class and a new art without breeding and without ancestry, and set this art and this class between the hut and the castle, and between the hut and the cloister, the art of the people was as closely mingled with the art of the coteries as was the speech of the people that delighted in rhythmical animation, in idiom, in images, in words full of far-off suggestion, with the unchanging speech of the poets.

Now I see a new generation in Ireland which discusses Irish literature and history in Young Ireland societies, and societies with newer names, and there are far more than when I was a boy who would make verses for the people. They have the help, too, of a vigorous journalism, and this journalism sometimes urges them to desire the direct logic, the clear rhetoric, of 'popular poetry.' It sees that Ireland has no cultivated minority, and it does not see, though it would cast out all English things, that its literary ideal belongs more to England than to other countries. I have hope that the new writers will not fall into its illusion, for they write in Irish, and for a people the counting-house has not made forgetful. Among the seven or eight hundred thousand who have had Irish from the cradle, there is, perhaps, nobody who has not enough of the unwritten tradition to know good verses from bad ones, if he have enough mother-wit. Among all that speak English in Australia, in America, in Great Britain, are there many more than the ten thousand the prophet saw, who have enough of the written tradition education has set in room of the unwritten to know good verses from bad ones, even though their mother-wit has made them Ministers of the Crown or what you will? Nor can things be better till that ten thousand have gone hither and thither to preach their faith that 'the imagination is the man himself,' and that the world as imagination sees it is the durable world, and have won men as did the disciples of Him who—

His seventy disciples sent
Against religion and government.

1901

Speaking to the Psaltery

I

I HAVE ALWAYS KNOWN THAT there was something I disliked about singing, and I naturally dislike print and paper, but now at last I understand why, for I have found something better. I have just heard a poem spoken with so delicate a sense of its rhythm, with so perfect a respect for its meaning, that if I were a wise man and could persuade a few people to learn the art I would never open a book of verses again. A friend, who was here a few minutes ago, has sat with a beautiful stringed instrument upon her knee, her fingers passing over the strings, and has spoken to me some verses from Shelley's *Skylark* and Sir Ector's lamentation over the dead Launcelot out of the *Morte d'Arthur* and some of my own poems. Wherever the rhythm was most delicate, wherever the emotion was most ecstatic, her art was the most beautiful, and yet, although she sometimes spoke to a little tune, it was never singing, as we sing to-day, never anything but speech. A singing note, a word chanted as they chant in churches, would have spoiled everything; nor was it reciting, for she spoke to a notation as definite as that of song, using the instrument, which murmured sweetly and faintly, under the spoken sounds, to give her the changing notes. Another speaker could have repeated all her effects, except those which came from her own beautiful voice that would have given her fame if the only art that gives the speaking voice its perfect opportunity were as well known among us as it was known in the ancient world.

II

SINCE I WAS A BOY I have always longed to hear poems spoken to a harp, as I imagined Homer to have spoken his, for it is not natural to enjoy an art only when one is by oneself. Whenever one finds a fine verse one wants to read it to somebody, and it would be much less trouble and much pleasanter if we could all listen, friend by friend, lover by beloved. Images used to rise up before me, as I am sure they have arisen before nearly everybody else who cares for poetry, of wild-eyed men speaking harmoniously to murmuring wires while audiences in many-coloured robes listened, hushed and excited. Whenever I spoke of my desire to anybody they said I should write for music, but when I heard anything sung I did not hear the words, or if I did their natural pronunciation was altered and their natural music was altered, or it was drowned in another music which I did not understand. What was the good of writing a love-song if the singer pronounced love, 'lo-o-o-o-o-ve,' or even if he said 'love,' but did not give it its exact place and weight in the rhythm? Like every other poet, I spoke verses in a kind of chant when I was making them, and sometimes, when I was alone on a country road, I would speak them in a loud chanting voice, and feel that if I dared I would speak them in that way to other people. One day I was walking through a Dublin street with the Visionary I have written about in *The Celtic Twilight*, and he began speaking his verses out aloud with the confidence of those who have the inner light. He did not mind that people stopped and looked after him even on the far side of the road, but went on through poem after poem. Like myself, he knew nothing of music, but was certain that he had written them to a manner of music, and he had once asked somebody who played on a wind instrument of some kind, and then a violinist, to write out the music and play it. The violinist had played it, or something like it, but had not written it down; but the man with the wind instrument said it could not be played because it contained quarter-tones and would be out of tune. We were not at all convinced by this, and one day, when we were staying with a Galway friend who is a learned musician, I asked him to listen to our verses, and to the way we spoke them. The Visionary found to his surprise that he did not make every poem to a different tune, and to the surprise of the musician that he did make them all to two quite definite tunes, which are, it seems, like very simple Arabic music. It was, perhaps, to some such music, I thought, that Blake sang his *Songs of Innocence* in Mrs. Williams' drawing-room, and perhaps he, too, spoke rather than sang. I, on the other hand, did not often compose to a tune, though I sometimes did, yet always to notes that could be written down and played on my friend's organ, or turned into something like a Gregorian hymn if one sang them in the ordinary way. I varied more than the Visionary, who never forgot his two tunes, one for long and one for short lines, and could not always speak a poem in the same way, but always felt that certain ways were right, and that I would know one of them if I remembered the way I first spoke the poem. When I got to London I gave the notation, as it had been played on the organ, to the friend who has just gone out, and she spoke it to me, giving my words a new quality by the beauty of her voice.

III

THEN WE BEGAN TO WANDER through the wood of error; we tried speaking through music in the ordinary way under I know not whose evil influence, until we got to hate the two competing tunes and rhythms that were so often at discord with one another, the tune and rhythm of the verse and the tune and rhythm of the music. Then we tried, persuaded by somebody who thought quarter-tones and less intervals the especial mark of speech as distinct from singing, to write out what we did in wavy lines. On finding something like these lines in Tibetan music, we became so confident that we covered a large piece of pasteboard, which now blows up my fire in the morning, with a notation in wavy lines as a demonstration for a lecture; but at last Mr. Dolmetsch put us back to our first thought. He made us a beautiful instrument half psaltery half lyre which contains, I understand, all the chromatic intervals within the range of the speaking voice; and he taught us to regulate our speech by the ordinary musical notes.

Some of the notations he taught us—those in which there is no lilt, no recurring pattern of sounds—are like this notation for a song out of the first Act of *The Countess Cathleen*.

It is written in the old C clef, which is, I am told, the most reasonable way to write it, for it would be below the stave on the treble clef or above it on the bass clef. The central line of the stave corresponds to the middle C of the piano; the first note of the poem is therefore D. The marks of long and short over the syllables are not marks of scansion, but show the syllables one makes the voice hurry or linger over.

One needs, of course, a far less complicated notation than a singer, and one is even permitted slight modifications of the fixed note when dramatic expression demands it and the instrument is not sounding. The notation which regulates the general form of the sound leaves it free to add a complexity of dramatic expression from its own incommunicable genius which compensates the lover of speech for the lack of complex musical expression. Ordinary speech is formless, and its variety is like the variety which separates bad prose from the regulated speech of Milton, or anything that is formless and void from anything that has form and beauty. The orator, the speaker who has some little of the great tradition of his craft, differs from the debater very largely because he understands how to assume that subtle monotony of voice which runs through the nerves like fire.

Even when one is speaking to a single note sounded faintly on the Psaltery, if one is sufficiently practised to speak on it without thinking about it one can get an endless variety of expression. All art is, indeed, a monotony in external things for the sake of an interior variety, a sacrifice of gross effects to subtle effects, an asceticism of the imagination. But this new art, new in modern life I mean, will have to train its hearers as well as its speakers, for it takes time to surrender gladly the gross efforts one is accustomed to, and one may well find mere monotony at first where one soon learns to find a variety as incalculable as in the outline of faces or in the expression of eyes. Modern acting and recitation have taught us to fix our attention on the gross effects till we have come to think gesture and the intonation that copies the accidental surface of life more important than the rhythm; and yet we understand theoretically that it is precisely this rhythm that separates good writing from bad, that is the glimmer, the fragrance, the spirit of all intense literature. I do not say that we should speak our plays to musical notes, for dramatic verse will need its own method, and I have hitherto experimented with short lyric poems alone; but I am certain that, if people would listen for a while to lyrical verse spoken to notes, they would soon find it impossible to listen without indignation to verse as it is spoken in our leading theatres. They would get a subtlety of hearing that would demand new effects from actors and even from public speakers, and they might, it may be, begin even to notice one another's voices till poetry and rhythm had come nearer to common life.

I cannot tell what changes this new art is to go through, or to what greatness or littleness of fortune; but I can imagine little stories in prose with their dialogues in metre going pleasantly to the strings. I am not certain that I shall not see some Order naming itself from the Golden Violet of the Troubadours or the like, and having among its members none but well-taught and well-mannered speakers who will keep the new art from disrepute. They will know how to keep from singing notes and from prosaic lifeless intonations, and they will always understand, however far they push their experiments, that poetry and not music is their object; and they will have by heart, like the Irish *File*, so many poems and notations that they will never have to bend their heads over the book to the ruin of dramatic expression and of that wild air the bard had always about him in my boyish imagination. They will go here and there speaking their verses and their little stories wherever they can find a score or two of poetical-minded people in a big room, or a couple of poetical-minded friends sitting by the hearth, and poets will write them poems and little stories to the confounding of print and paper. I, at any rate, from this out mean to write all my longer poems for the stage, and all my shorter ones for the Psaltery, if only some strong angel keep me to my good resolutions.

1902

Magic

I

I BELIEVE IN THE PRACTICE and philosophy of what we have agreed to call magic, in what I must call the evocation of spirits, though I do not know what they are, in the power of creating magical illusions, in the visions of truth in the depths of the mind when the eyes are closed; and I believe in three doctrines, which have, as I think, been handed down from early times, and been the foundations of nearly all magical practices. These doctrines are—

(1) That the borders of our minds are ever shifting, and that many minds can flow into one another, as it were, and create or reveal a single mind, a single energy.
(2) That the borders of our memories are as shifting, and that our memories are a part of one great memory, the memory of Nature herself.
(3) That this great mind and great memory can be evoked by symbols.

I often think I would put this belief in magic from me if I could, for I have come to see or to imagine, in men and women, in houses, in handicrafts, in nearly all sights and sounds, a certain evil, a certain ugliness, that comes from the slow perishing through the centuries of a quality of mind that made this belief and its evidences common over the world.

II

SOME TEN OR TWELVE YEARS ago, a man with whom I have since quarrelled for sound reasons, a very singular man who had given his life to studies other men despised, asked me and an acquaintance, who is now dead, to witness a magical work. He lived a little way from London, and on the way my acquaintance told me that he did not believe in magic, but that a novel of Bulwer Lytton's had taken such a hold upon his imagination that he was going to give much of his time and all his thought to magic. He longed to believe in it, and had studied, though not learnedly, geomancy, astrology, chiromancy, and much cabalistic symbolism, and yet doubted if the soul outlived the body. He awaited the magical work full of scepticism. He expected nothing more than an air of romance, an illusion as of the stage, that might capture the consenting imagination for an hour. The evoker of spirits and his beautiful wife received us in a little house, on the edge of some kind of garden or park belonging to an eccentric rich man, whose curiosities he arranged and dusted, and he made his evocation in a long room that had a raised place on the floor at one end, a kind of dais, but was furnished meagrely and cheaply. I sat with my acquaintance in the middle of the room, and the evoker of spirits on the dais, and his wife between us and him. He held a wooden mace in his hand, and turning to a tablet of many-coloured squares, with a number on each of the squares, that stood near him on a chair, he repeated a form of words. Almost at once my imagination began to move of itself and to bring before me vivid images that, though never too vivid to be imagination, as I had always understood it, had yet a motion of their own, a life I could not change or shape. I remember seeing a number of white figures, and wondering whether their mitred heads had been suggested by the mitred head of the mace, and then, of a sudden, the image of my acquaintance in the midst of them. I told what I had seen, and the evoker of spirits cried in a deep voice, 'Let him be blotted out,' and as he said it the image of my acquaintance vanished, and the evoker of spirits or his wife saw a man dressed in black with a curious square cap standing among the white figures. It was my acquaintance, the seeress said, as he had been in a past life, the life that had moulded his present, and that life would now unfold before us. I too seemed to see the man with a strange vividness. The story unfolded itself chiefly before the mind's eye of the seeress, but sometimes I saw what she described before I heard her description. She thought the man in black was perhaps a Fleming of the sixteenth century, and I could see him pass along narrow streets till he came to a narrow door with some rusty ironwork above it. He went in, and wishing to find out how far we had one vision among us, I kept silent when I saw a dead body lying upon the table within the door. The seeress described him going down a long hall and up into what she called a pulpit, and beginning to speak. She said, 'He is a clergyman, I can hear his words. They sound like Low Dutch.' Then after a little silence, 'No, I am wrong. I can see the listeners; he is a doctor lecturing among his pupils.' I said, 'Do you see anything near the door?' and she said, 'Yes, I see a subject for dissection.' Then we saw him go out again into the narrow streets, I following the story of the seeress, sometimes merely following her words, but sometimes seeing for myself. My acquaintance saw nothing; I think he was forbidden to see, it being his own life, and I think could not in any case. His imagination had no will of its own. Presently the man in black went into a house with two gables facing the road, and up some stairs into a room where a hump-backed woman gave him a key; and then along a corridor, and down some stairs into a large cellar full of retorts and strange vessels of all kinds. Here he seemed to stay a long while, and one saw him eating bread that he took down from a shelf. The evoker of spirits and the seeress began to speculate about the man's character and habits, and decided, from a visionary impression, that his mind was absorbed in naturalism, but that his imagination had been excited by stories of the marvels wrought by magic in past times, and that he was trying to copy them by naturalistic means. Presently one of them saw him go to a vessel that stood over a slow fire, and take out of the vessel a thing wrapped up in numberless cloths, which he partly unwrapped, showing at length what looked like the image of a man made by somebody who could not model. The evoker of spirits said that the man in black was trying to make flesh by chemical means, and though he had not succeeded, his brooding had drawn so many evil spirits about him, that the image was partly alive. He could see it moving a little where it lay upon a table. At that moment I heard something like little squeals, but kept silent, as when I saw the dead body. In a moment more the seeress said, 'I hear little squeals.' Then the evoker of spirits heard them, but said, 'They are not squeals; he is pouring a red liquid out of a retort through a slit in the cloth; the slit is over the mouth of the image and the liquid is gurgling in rather a curious way.' Weeks seemed to pass by hurriedly, and somebody saw the man still busy in his cellar. Then more weeks seemed to pass, and now we saw him lying sick in a room up-stairs, and a man in a conical cap standing beside him. We could see the image too. It was in the cellar, but now it could move feebly about the floor. I saw fainter images of the image passing continually from where it crawled to the man in his bed, and I asked the evoker of spirits what they were. He said, 'They are the images of his terror.' Presently the man in the conical cap began to speak, but who heard him I cannot remember. He made the sick man get out of bed and walk, leaning upon him, and in much terror till they came to the cellar. There the man in the conical cap made some symbol over the image, which fell back as if asleep, and putting a knife into the other's hand he said, 'I have taken from it the magical life, but you must take from it the life you gave.' Somebody saw

WILLIAM BUTLER YEATS

the sick man stoop and sever the head of the image from its body, and then fall as if he had given himself a mortal wound, for he had filled it with his own life. And then the vision changed and fluttered, and he was lying sick again in the room up-stairs. He seemed to lie there a long time with the man in the conical cap watching beside him, and then, I cannot remember how, the evoker of spirits discovered that though he would in part recover, he would never be well, and that the story had got abroad in the town and shattered his good name. His pupils had left him and men avoided him. He was accursed. He was a magician.

The story was finished, and I looked at my acquaintance. He was white and awestruck. He said, as nearly as I can remember, 'All my life I have seen myself in dreams making a man by some means like that. When I was a child I was always thinking out contrivances for galvanizing a corpse into life.' Presently he said, 'Perhaps my bad health in this life comes from that experiment.' I asked if he had read *Frankenstein*, and he answered that he had. He was the only one of us who had, and he had taken no part in the vision.

III

THEN I ASKED TO HAVE some past life of mine revealed, and a new evocation was made before the tablet full of little squares. I cannot remember so well who saw this or that detail, for now I was interested in little but the vision itself. I had come to a conclusion about the method. I knew that the vision may be in part common to several people.

A man in chain armour passed through a castle door, and the seeress noticed with surprise the bareness and rudeness of castle rooms. There was nothing of the magnificence or the pageantry she had expected. The man came to a large hall and to a little chapel opening out of it, where a ceremony was taking place. There were six girls dressed in white, who took from the altar some yellow object—I thought it was gold, for though, like my acquaintance, I was told not to see, I could not help seeing. Somebody else thought that it was yellow flowers, and I think the girls, though I cannot remember clearly, laid it between the man's hands. He went out after a time, and as he passed through the great hall one of us, I forget whom, noticed that he passed over two gravestones. Then the vision became broken, but presently he stood in a monk's habit among men-at-arms in the middle of a village reading from a parchment. He was calling villagers about him, and presently he and they and the men-at-arms took ship for some long voyage. The vision became broken again, and when we could see clearly they had come to what seemed the Holy Land. They had begun some kind of sacred labour among palm-trees. The common men among them stood idle, but the gentlemen carried large stones, bringing them from certain directions, from the cardinal points I think, with a ceremonious formality. The evoker of spirits said they must be making some kind of masonic house. His mind, like the minds of so many students of these hidden things, was always running on masonry and discovering it in strange places.

We broke the vision that we might have supper, breaking it with some form of words which I forget. When supper had ended the seeress cried out that while we had been eating they had been building, and they had built not a masonic house but a great stone cross. And now they had all gone away but the man who had been in chain armour and two monks we had not noticed before. He was standing against the cross, his feet upon two stone rests a little above the ground, and his arms spread out. He seemed to stand there all day, but when night came he went to a little cell, that was beside two other cells. I think they were like the cells I have seen in the Aran Islands, but I cannot be certain. Many days seemed to pass, and all day every day he stood upon the cross, and we never saw anybody there but him and the two monks. Many years seemed to pass, making the vision flutter like a drift of leaves before our eyes, and he grew old and white-haired, and we saw the two monks, old and white-haired, holding him upon the cross. I asked the evoker of spirits why the man stood there, and before he had time to answer I saw two people, a man and a woman, rising like a dream within a dream, before the eyes of the man upon the cross. The evoker of spirits saw them too, and said that one of them held up his arms and they were without hands. I thought of the two gravestones the man in chain mail had passed over in the great hall when he came out of the chapel, and asked the evoker of spirits if the knight was undergoing a penance for violence, and while I was asking him, and he was saying that it might be so but he did not know, the vision, having completed its circle, vanished.

It had not, so far as I could see, the personal significance of the other vision, but it was certainly strange and beautiful, though I alone seemed to see its beauty. Who was it that made the story, if it were but a story? I did not, and the seeress did not, and the evoker of spirits did not and could not. It arose in three minds, for I cannot remember my acquaintance taking any part, and it rose without confusion, and without labour, except the labour of keeping the mind's eye awake, and more swiftly than any pen could have written it out. It may be, as Blake said of one of his poems, that the author was in eternity. In coming years I was to see and hear of many such visions, and though I was not to be convinced, though half convinced once or twice, that they were old lives, in an ordinary sense of the word life, I was to learn that they have almost always some quite definite relation to dominant moods and moulding events in this life. They are, perhaps, in most cases, though the vision I have but just described was not, it seems, among the cases, symbolical histories of these moods and events, or rather symbolical shadows of the impulses that have made them, messages as it were out of the ancestral being of the questioner.

At the time these two visions meant little more to me, if I can remember my feeling at the time, than a proof of the supremacy of imagination, of the power of many minds to become one, overpowering one another by spoken words and by unspoken thought till they have become a single intense, unhesitating energy. One mind was doubtless the master, I thought, but all the minds gave a little, creating or revealing for a moment what I must call a supernatural artist.

IV

SOME YEARS AFTERWARDS I WAS staying with some friends in Paris. I had got up before breakfast and gone out to buy a newspaper. I had noticed the servant, a girl who had come from the country some years before, laying the table for breakfast. As I had passed her I had been telling myself one of those long foolish tales which one tells only to oneself. If something had happened that had not happened, I would have hurt my arm, I thought. I saw myself with my arm in a sling in the middle of some childish adventures. I returned with the newspaper and met my host and hostess in the door. The moment they saw me they cried out, 'Why, the *bonne* has just told us you had your arm in a sling. We thought something must have happened to you last night, that you had been run over maybe'—or some such words. I had been dining out at the other end of Paris, and had come in after everybody had gone to bed. I had cast my imagination so strongly upon the servant that she had seen it, and with what had appeared to be more than the mind's eye.

One afternoon, about the same time, I was thinking very intently of a certain fellow-student for whom I had a message, which I hesitated about writing. In a couple of days I got a letter from a place some hundreds of miles away where that student was. On the afternoon when I had been thinking so intently I had suddenly appeared there amid a crowd of people in a hotel and as seeming solid as if in the flesh. My fellow-student had seen me, but no one else, and had asked me to come again when the people had gone. I had vanished, but had come again in the middle of the night and given the message. I myself had no knowledge of casting an imagination upon one so far away.

I could tell of stranger images, of stranger enchantments, of stranger imaginations, cast consciously or unconsciously over as great distances by friends or by myself, were it not that the greater energies of the mind seldom break forth but when the deeps are loosened. They break forth amid events too private or too sacred for public speech, or seem themselves, I know not why, to belong to hidden things. I have written of these breakings forth, these loosenings of the deep, with some care and some detail, but I shall keep my record shut. After all, one can but bear witness less to convince him who won't believe than to protect him who does, as Blake puts it, enduring unbelief and misbelief and ridicule as best one may. I shall be content to show that past times have believed as I do, by quoting Joseph Glanvil's description of the Scholar Gipsy. Joseph Glanvil is dead, and will not mind unbelief and misbelief and ridicule.

The Scholar Gipsy, too, is dead, unless indeed perfectly wise magicians can live till it please them to die, and he is wandering somewhere, even if one cannot see him, as Arnold imagined, 'at some lone ale-house in the Berkshire moors, on the warm ingle-bench,' or 'crossing the stripling Thames at Bablock Hithe,' 'trailing his fingers in the cool stream,' or 'giving store of flowers—the frail-leaf'd white anemone, dark hare-bells drenched with dew of summer eves,' to the girls 'who from the distant hamlets come to dance around the Fyfield elm in May,' or 'sitting upon the river bank o'ergrown,' living on through time 'with a free onward impulse.' This is Joseph Glanvil's story—

> There was very lately a lad in the University of Oxford who, being of very pregnant and ready parts and yet wanting the encouragement of preferment, was by his poverty forced to leave his studies there, and to cast himself upon the wide world for a livelihood. Now his necessities growing daily on him, and wanting

the help of friends to relieve him, he was at last forced to join himself to a company of vagabond gipsies, whom occasionally he met with, and to follow their trade for a maintenance. . . After he had been a pretty while well exercised in the trade, there chanced to ride by a couple of scholars, who had formerly been of his acquaintance. The scholar had quickly spied out these old friends among the gipsies, and their amazement to see him among such society had well-nigh discovered him; but by a sign he prevented them owning him before that crew, and taking one of them aside privately, desired him with his friend to go to an inn, not far distant, promising there to come to them. They accordingly went thither and he follows: after their first salutation his friends inquire how he came to lead so odd a life as that was, and so joined himself into such a beggarly company. The scholar gipsy having given them an account of the necessity which drove him to that kind of life, told them that the people he went with were not such impostors as they were taken for, but that they had a traditional kind of learning among them and could do wonders by the power of imagination, and that himself had learned much of their art and improved it further than themselves could. And to evince the truth of what he told them, he said he'd remove into another room, leaving them to discourse together; and upon his return tell them the sense of what they had talked of; which accordingly he performed, giving them a full account of what had passed between them in his absence. The scholars being amazed at so unexpected a discovery, earnestly desired him to unriddle the mystery. In which he gave them satisfaction, by telling them that what he did was by the power of imagination, his phantasy leading theirs; and that himself had dictated to them the discourse they had held together while he was from them; that there were warrantable ways of heightening the imagination to that pitch as to bend another's, and that when he had compassed the whole secret, some parts of which he was yet ignorant of, he intended to leave their company and give the world an account of what he had learned.

If all who have described events like this have not dreamed, we should rewrite our histories, for all men, certainly all imaginative men, must be for ever casting forth enchantments, glamours, illusions; and all men, especially tranquil men who have no powerful egotistic life, must be continually passing under their power. Our most elaborate thoughts, elaborate purposes, precise emotions, are often, as I think, not really ours, but have on a sudden come up, as it were, out of hell or down out of heaven. The historian should remember, should he not? angels and devils not less than kings and soldiers, and plotters and thinkers. What matter if the angel or devil, as indeed certain old writers believed, first wrapped itself with an organized shape in some man's imagination? what matter 'if God himself only acts or is in existing beings or men,' as Blake believed? we must none the less admit that invisible beings, far wandering influences, shapes that may have floated from a hermit of the wilderness, brood over council-chambers and studies and battle-fields. We should never be certain that it was not some woman treading in the wine-press who began that subtle change in men's minds, that powerful movement of thought and imagination about which so many Germans have written; or that the passion, because of which so many countries were given to the sword, did not begin in the mind of some shepherd boy, lighting up his eyes for a moment before it ran upon its way.

V

WE CANNOT DOUBT THAT BARBARIC people receive such influences more visibly and obviously, and in all likelihood more easily and fully than we do, for our life in cities, which deafens or kills the passive meditative life, and our education that enlarges the separated, self-moving mind, have made our souls less sensitive. Our souls that were once naked to the winds of heaven are now thickly clad, and have learned to build a house and light a fire upon its hearth, and shut to the doors and windows. The winds can, indeed, make us draw near to the fire, or can even lift the carpet and whistle under the door, but they could do worse out on the plains long ago. A certain learned man, quoted by Mr. Lang in his *Making of Religion*, contends that the memories of primitive man and his thoughts of distant places must have had the intensity of hallucination, because there was nothing in his mind to draw his attention away from them—an explanation that does not seem to me complete—and Mr. Lang goes on to quote certain travellers to prove that savages live always on the edges of vision. One Laplander who wished to become a Christian, and thought visions but heathenish, confessed to a traveller, to whom he had given a minute account of many distant events, read doubtless in that traveller's mind, 'that he knew not how to make use of his eyes, since things altogether distant were present to them.' I myself could find in one district in Galway but one man who had not seen what I can but call spirits, and he was in his dotage. 'There is no man mowing a meadow but sees them at one time or another,' said a man in a different district.

If I can unintentionally cast a glamour, an enchantment, over persons of our own time who have lived for years in great cities, there is no reason to doubt that men could cast intentionally a far stronger enchantment, a far stronger glamour, over the more sensitive people of ancient times, or that men can still do so where the old order of life remains unbroken. Why should not the Scholar Gipsy cast his spell over his friends? Why should not St. Patrick, or he of whom the story was first told, pass his enemies, he and all his clerics, as a herd of deer? Why should not enchanters like him in the *Morte d'Arthur* make troops of horse seem but grey stones? Why should not the Roman soldiers, though they came of a civilization which was ceasing to be sensitive to these things, have trembled for a moment before the enchantments of the Druids of Mona? Why should not the Jesuit father, or the Count Saint Germain, or whoever the tale was first told of, have really seemed to leave the city in a coach and four by all the Twelve Gates at once? Why should not Moses and the enchanters of Pharaoh have made their staffs as the medicine men of many primitive peoples make their pieces of old rope seem like devouring serpents? Why should not that mediæval enchanter have made summer and all its blossoms seem to break forth in middle winter?

May we not learn some day to rewrite our histories, when they touch upon these things too?

Men who are imaginative writers to-day may well have preferred to influence the imagination of others more directly in past times. Instead of learning their craft with paper and a pen they may have sat for hours imagining themselves to be stocks and stones and beasts of the wood, till the images were so vivid that the passers-by became but a part of the imagination of the dreamer, and wept or laughed or ran away as he would have them. Have not poetry and music arisen, as it seems, out of the sounds the enchanters made to help their imagination to enchant, to charm, to bind with a spell themselves and the passers-by? These very words, a chief part of all praises of music or poetry, still cry to us their origin. And just as the musician or the poet enchants and charms and binds with a spell his own mind when he would enchant the mind of others, so did the enchanter create or reveal for himself as well as for others the supernatural artist or genius, the seeming transitory mind made out of many minds, whose work I saw, or thought I saw, in that suburban house. He kept the doors too, as it seems, of those less transitory minds, the genius of the family, the genius of the tribe, or it may be, when he was mighty-souled enough, the genius of the world. Our history speaks of opinions and discoveries, but in ancient times when, as I think, men had their eyes ever upon those doors, history spoke of commandments and revelations. They looked as carefully and as patiently towards Sinai and its thunders as we look towards parliaments and laboratories. We are always praising men in whom the individual life has come to perfection, but they were always praising the one mind, their foundation of all perfection.

VI

I ONCE SAW A YOUNG Irish woman, fresh from a convent school, cast into a profound trance, though not by a method known to any hypnotist. In her waking state she thought the apple of Eve was the kind of apple you can buy at the greengrocer's, but in her trance she saw the Tree of Life with ever-sighing souls moving in its branches instead of sap, and among its leaves all the fowl of the air, and on its highest bough one white fowl bearing a crown. When I went home I took from the shelf a translation of *The Book of Concealed Mystery*, an old Jewish book, and cutting the pages came upon this passage, which I cannot think I had ever read: 'The Tree, . . . is the Tree of the Knowledge of Good and of Evil. . . in its branches the birds lodge and build their nests, the souls and the angels have their place.'

I once saw a young Church of Ireland man, a bank clerk in the west of Ireland, thrown in a like trance. I have no doubt that he, too, was quite certain that the apple of Eve was a greengrocer's apple, and yet he saw the tree and heard the souls sighing through its branches, and saw apples with human faces, and laying his ear to an apple heard a sound as of fighting hosts within. Presently he strayed from the tree and came to the edge of Eden, and there he found himself not by the wilderness he had learned of at the Sunday-school, but upon the summit of a great mountain, of a mountain 'two miles high.' The whole summit, in contradiction to all that would have seemed probable to his waking mind, was a great walled garden. Some years afterwards I found a mediæval diagram, which pictured Eden as a walled garden upon a high mountain.

Where did these intricate symbols come from? Neither I nor the one or two people present or the seers had ever seen, I am convinced, the description in *The Book of Concealed Mystery*, or the mediæval diagram. Remember that the images appeared in a moment perfect in all their complexity. If one can imagine that the seers or that I myself or another had indeed read of these images and forgotten it, that the supernatural artist's knowledge of what was in our buried memories accounted for these visions, there are numberless other visions to account for. One cannot go on believing in improbable knowledge for ever. For instance, I find in my diary that on December 27, 1897, a seer, to whom I had given a certain old Irish symbol, saw Brigit, the goddess, holding out 'a glittering and wriggling serpent,' and yet I feel certain that neither I nor he knew anything of her association with the serpent until *Carmina Gadelica* was published a few months ago. And an old Irish woman who can neither read nor write has described to me a woman dressed like Dian, with helmet, and short skirt and sandals, and what seemed to be buskins. Why, too, among all the countless stories of visions that I have gathered in Ireland, or that a friend has gathered for me, are there none that mix the dress of different periods? The seers when they are but speaking from tradition will mix everything together, and speak of Finn mac Cool going to the Assizes at Cork. Almost every one who has ever busied himself with such matters has come, in trance or dream, upon some new and strange symbol or event, which he has afterwards found in some work he had never read or heard of. Examples like this are as yet too little classified, too little analyzed, to convince the stranger, but some of them are proof enough for those they have happened to, proof that there is a memory of nature that reveals events and symbols of distant centuries. Mystics of many countries and many centuries have spoken of this memory; and the honest men and charlatans, who keep the magical traditions which will some day be studied as a part of folk-lore, base most that is of importance in their claims upon this memory. I have read of it in 'Paracelsus' and in some Indian book that describes the people of past days as still living within it, 'Thinking the thought and doing the deed.' And I have found it in the prophetic books of William Blake, who calls its images 'the bright sculptures of Los's Halls'; and says that all events, 'all love stories,' renew themselves from those images. It is perhaps well that so few believe in it, for if many did many would go out of parliaments and universities and libraries and run into the wilderness to so waste the body, and to so hush the unquiet mind that, still living, they might pass the doors the dead pass daily; for who among the wise would trouble himself with making laws or in writing history or in weighing the earth if the things of eternity seemed ready to hand?

VII

I FIND IN MY DIARY of magical events for 1899 that I awoke at 3 A.M. out of a nightmare, and imagined one symbol to prevent its recurrence, and imagined another, a simple geometrical form, which calls up dreams of luxuriant vegetable life, that I might have pleasant dreams. I imagined it faintly, being very sleepy, and went to sleep. I had confused dreams which seemed to have no relation with the symbol. I awoke about eight, having for the time forgotten both nightmare and symbol. Presently I dozed off again and began half to dream and half to see, as one does between sleep and waking, enormous flowers and grapes. I awoke and recognized that what I had dreamed or seen was the kind of thing appropriate to the symbol before I remembered having used it. I find another record, though made some time after the event, of having imagined over the head of a person, who was a little of a seer, a combined symbol of elemental air and elemental water. This person, who did not know what symbol I was using, saw a pigeon flying with a lobster in his bill. I find that on December 13, 1898, I used a certain star-shaped symbol with a seeress, getting her to look at it intently before she began seeing. She saw a rough stone house, and in the middle of the house the skull of a horse. I find that I had used the same symbol a few days before with a seer, and that he had seen a rough stone house, and in the middle of the house something under a cloth marked with the Hammer of Thor. He had lifted the cloth and discovered a skeleton of gold with teeth of diamonds, and eyes of some unknown dim precious stones. I had made a note to this last vision, pointing out that we had been using a Solar symbol a little earlier. Solar symbols often call up visions of gold and precious stones. I do not give these examples to prove my arguments, but to illustrate them. I know that my examples will awaken in all who have not met the like, or who are not on other grounds inclined towards my arguments, a most natural incredulity. It was long before I myself would admit an inherent power in symbols, for it long seemed to me that one could account for everything by the power of one imagination over another, telepathy as it is called with that separation of knowledge and life, of word and emotion, which is the sterility of scientific speech. The symbol seemed powerful, I thought, merely because we thought it powerful, and we would do just as well without it. In those days I used symbols made with some ingenuity instead of merely imagining them. I used to give them to the person I was experimenting with, and tell him to hold them to his forehead without looking at them; and sometimes I made a mistake. I learned from these mistakes that if I did not myself imagine the symbol, in which case he would have a mixed vision, it was the symbol I gave by mistake that produced the vision. Then I met with a seer who could say to me, 'I have a vision of a square pond, but I can see your thought, and you expect me to see an oblong pond,' or, 'The symbol you are imagining has made me see a woman holding a crystal, but it was a moonlight sea I should have seen.' I discovered that the symbol hardly ever failed to call up its typical scene, its typical event, its typical person, but that I could practically never call up, no matter how vividly I imagined it, the particular scene, the particular event, the particular person I had in my own mind, and that when I could, the two visions rose side by side.

I cannot now think symbols less than the greatest of all powers whether they are used consciously by the masters of magic, or half unconsciously by their successors, the poet, the musician and the artist. At first I tried to distinguish between symbols and symbols, between what I called inherent symbols and arbitrary symbols, but the distinction has come to mean little or nothing. Whether their power has arisen out of themselves, or whether it has an arbitrary origin, matters little, for they act, as I believe, because the great memory associates them with certain events and moods and persons. Whatever the passions of man have gathered about, becomes a symbol in the great memory, and in the hands of him who has the secret, it is a worker of wonders, a caller-up of angels or of devils. The symbols are of all kinds, for everything in heaven or earth has its association, momentous or trivial, in the great memory, and one never knows what forgotten events may have plunged it, like the toadstool and the ragweed, into the great passions. Knowledgeable men and women in Ireland sometimes distinguish between the simples that work cures by some medical property in the herb, and those that do their work by magic. Such magical simples as the husk of the flax, water out of the fork of an elm-tree, do their work, as I think, by awaking in the depths of the mind where it mingles with the great mind, and is enlarged by the great memory, some curative energy, some hypnotic command. They are not what we call faith cures, for they have been much used and successfully, the traditions of all lands affirm, over children and over animals, and to me they seem the only medicine that could have been committed safely to ancient hands. To pluck the wrong leaf would have been to go uncured, but, if one had eaten it, one might have been poisoned.

VIII

I HAVE NOW DESCRIBED THAT belief in magic which has set me all but unwilling among those lean and fierce minds who are at war with their time, who cannot accept the days as they pass, simply and gladly; and I look at what I have written with some alarm, for I have told more of the ancient secret than many among my fellow-students think it right to tell. I have come to believe so many strange things because of experience, that I see little reason to doubt the truth of many things that are beyond my experience; and it may be that there are beings who watch over that ancient secret, as all tradition affirms, and resent, and perhaps avenge, too fluent speech. They say in the Aran Islands that if you speak overmuch of the things of Faery your tongue becomes like a stone, and it seems to me, though doubtless naturalistic reason would call it Auto-suggestion or the like, that I have often felt my tongue become just so heavy and clumsy. More than once, too, as I wrote this very essay I have become uneasy, and have torn up some paragraph, not for any literary reason, but because some incident or some symbol that would perhaps have meant nothing to the reader, seemed, I know not why, to belong to hidden things. Yet I must write or be of no account to any cause, good or evil; I must commit what merchandise of wisdom I have to this ship of written speech, and after all, I have many a time watched it put out to sea with not less alarm when all the speech was rhyme. We who write, we who bear witness, must often hear our hearts cry out against us, complaining because of their hidden things, and I know not but he who speaks of wisdom may not sometimes in the change that is coming upon the world, have to fear the anger of the people of Faery, whose country is the heart of the world—'The Land of the Living Heart.' Who can keep always to the little pathway between speech and silence, where one meets none but discreet revelations? And surely, at whatever risk, we must cry out that imagination is always seeking to remake the world according to the impulses and the patterns in that great Mind, and that great Memory? Can there be anything so important as to cry out that what we call romance, poetry, intellectual beauty, is the only signal that the supreme Enchanter, or some one in His councils, is speaking of what has been, and shall be again, in the consummation of time?

1901

The Happiest of the Poets

I

Rossetti in one of his letters numbers his favourite colours in the order of his favour, and throughout his work one feels that he loved form and colour for themselves and apart from what they represent. One feels sometimes that he desired a world of essences, of unmixed powers, of impossible purities. It is as though the last judgment had already begun in his mind and that the essences and powers, which the divine hand had mixed into one another to make the loam of life, fell asunder at his touch. If he painted a flame or a blue distance, he painted as though he had seen the flame out of whose heart all flames had been taken, or the blue of the abyss that was before all life; and if he painted a woman's face he painted it in some moment of intensity when the ecstasy of the lover and of the saint are alike, and desire becomes wisdom without ceasing to be desire. He listens to the cry of the flesh till it becomes proud and passes beyond the world where some immense desire that the intellect cannot understand mixes with the desire of a body's warmth and softness. His genius like Shelley's can hardly stir but to the rejection of nature, whose delight is profusion, but never intensity, and like Shelley's it follows the Star of the Magi, the Morning and Evening Star, the mother of impossible hope, although it follows through deep woods, where the Star glimmers among dew-drenched boughs and not through 'a wind-swept valley of the Apennine.' Men like him cannot be happy as we understand happiness, for to be happy one must delight like nature in mere profusion, in mere abundance, in making and doing things, and if one sets an image of the perfect before one it must be the image that draws her perpetually, the image of a perfect fulness of natural life, of an Earthly Paradise. One's emotion must never break the bonds of life, one's hands must never labour to loosen the silver cord, one's ears must never strain to catch the sound of Michael's trumpet. That is to say, one must not be among those that would have prayed in old times in some chapel of the Star, but among those who would have prayed under the shadow of the Green Tree, and on the wet stones of the Well, among the worshippers of natural abundance.

I DO NOT THINK IT was accident, so subtle are the threads that lead the soul, that made William Morris, who seems to me the one perfectly happy and fortunate poet of modern times, celebrate the Green Tree and the goddess Habundia, and wells and enchanted waters in so many books. In *The Well at the World's End* green trees and enchanted waters are shown to us, as they were understood by old writers, who thought that the generation of all things was through water; for when the water that gives a long and a fortunate life and that can be found by none but such a one as all women love is found at last, the Dry Tree, the image of the ruined land, becomes green. To him indeed as to older writers Well and Tree are all but images of the one thing, of an 'energy' that is not the less 'eternal delight' because it is half of the body. He never wrote, and could not have written, of a man or woman who was not of the kin of Well or Tree. Long before he had named either he had made his 'Wanderers' follow a dream indeed, but a dream of natural happiness, and all the people of all his poems and stories from the confused beginning of his art in *The Hollow Land* to its end in *The Sundering Flood*, are full of the heavy sweetness of this dream. He wrote indeed of nothing but of the quest of the Grail, but it was the Heathen Grail that gave every man his chosen food, and not the Grail of Malory or Wagner; and he came at last to praise, as other men have praised the martyrs of religion or of passion, men with lucky eyes and men whom all women love.

We know so little of man and of the world that we cannot be certain that the same invisible hands, that gave him an imagination preoccupied with good fortune, gave him also health and wealth, and the power to create beautiful things without labour, that he might honour the Green Tree. It pleases me to imagine the copper mine which brought, as Mr. Mackail has told, so much unforeseen wealth and in so astonishing a way, as no less miraculous than the three arrows in *The Sundering Flood*. No mighty poet in his misery dead could have delighted enough to make us delight in men 'who knew no vain desire of foolish fame,' but who thought the dance upon 'the stubble field' and 'the battle with the earth' better than 'the bitter war' 'where right and wrong are mixed together.' 'Oh the trees, the trees!' he wrote in one of his early letters, and it was his work to make us, who had been taught to sympathize with the unhappy till we had grown morbid, to sympathize with men and women who turned everything into happiness because they had in them something of the abundance of the beechen boughs or of the bursting wheat-ear. He alone, I think, has told the story of Alcestis with perfect sympathy for Admetus, with so perfect a sympathy that he cannot persuade himself that one so happy died at all; and he, unlike all other poets, has delighted to tell us that the men after his own heart, the men of his *News from Nowhere*, sorrowed but a little while over unhappy love. He cannot even think of nobility and happiness apart, for all his people are like his men of Burg Dale who lived 'in much plenty and ease of life, though not delicately or desiring things out of measure. They wrought with their hands and wearied themselves; and they rested from their toil and feasted and were merry; to-morrow was not a burden to them, nor yesterday a thing which they would fain forget; life shamed them not nor did death make them afraid. As for the Dale wherein they dwelt, it was indeed most fair and lovely and they deemed it the Blessing of the earth, and they trod the flowery grass beside its rippled stream amidst the green tree-boughs proudly and joyfully with goodly bodies and merry hearts.'

III

I THINK OF HIS MEN as with broad brows and golden beards and mild eyes and tranquil speech, and of his good women as like 'The Bride' in whose face Rossetti saw and painted for once the abundance of earth and not the half-hidden light of his star. They are not in love with love for its own sake, with a love that is apart from the world or at enmity with it, as Swinburne imagines Mary Stuart and as all men have imagined Helen. They do not seek in love that ecstasy, which Shelley's nightingale called death, that extremity of life in which life seems to pass away like the Phoenix in flame of its own lighting, but rather a gentle self-surrender that would lose more than half its sweetness if it lost the savour of coming days. They are good house-wives; they sit often at the embroidery frame, and they have wisdom in flocks and herds and they are before all fruitful mothers. It seems at times as if their love was less a passion for one man out of the world than submission to the hazard of destiny, and the hope of motherhood and the innocent desire of the body. They accept changes and chances of life as gladly as they accept spring and summer and autumn and winter, and because they have sat under the shadow of the Green Tree and drunk the Waters of Abundance out of their hollow hands, the barren blossoms do not seem to them the most beautiful. When Habundia takes the shape of Birdalone she comes first as a young naked girl standing among great trees, and then as an old carline, Birdalone in stately old age. And when she praises Birdalone's naked body, and speaks of the desire it shall awaken, praise and desire are innocent because they would not break the links that chain the days to one another. The desire seems not other than the desire of the bird for its mate in the heart of the wood, and we listen to that joyous praise as though a bird watching its plumage in still water had begun to sing in its joy, or as if we heard hawk praising hawk in the middle air, and because it is the praise of one made for all noble life and not for pleasure only, it seems, though it is the praise of the body, that it is the noblest praise.

Birdalone has never seen her image but in 'a broad latten-dish,' so the wood woman must tell her of her body and praise it.

'Thus it is with thee; thou standest before me a tall and slim maiden, somewhat thin as befitteth thy seventeen summers; where thy flesh is bare of wont, as thy throat and thine arms and thy legs from the middle down, it is tanned a beauteous colour, but otherwhere it is even as fair a white, wholesome and clean as if the golden sunlight which fulfilleth the promise of the earth were playing therein. . . Delicate and clean-made is the little trench that goeth from thy mouth to thy lips, and sweet it is, and there is more might in it than in sweet words spoken. Thy lips they are of the finest fashion, yet rather thin than full; and some would not have it so; but I would, whereas I see therein a sign of thy valiancy and friendliness. Surely he who did thy carven chin had a mind to a master work and did no less. Great was the deftness of thine imaginer, and he would have all folk who see thee wonder at thy deep thinking and thy carefulness and thy kindness. Ah, maiden! is it so that thy thoughts are ever deep and solemn? Yet at least I know it of thee that they be hale and true and sweet.

'My friend, when thou hast a mirror, some of all this shalt thou see, but not all; and when thou hast a lover some deal wilt thou hear, but not all. But now thy she-friend may tell it thee all, if she have eyes to see it, as have I; whereas no man could say so much of thee before the mere love should overtake him, and turn his speech into the folly of love and the madness of desire.'

All his good women, whether it is Danaë in her tower, or that woman in *The Wood beyond the World* who can make the withered flowers in her girdle grow young again by the touch of her hand, are of the kin of the wood woman. All his bad women too and his half-bad women are of her kin. The evils their enchantments make are a disordered abundance like that of weedy places and they are cruel as wild creatures are cruel and they have unbridled desires. One finds these evils in their typical shape in that isle of the Wondrous Isles, where the wicked witch has her pleasure-house and her prison, and in that 'isle of the old and the young,' where until her enchantment is broken second childhood watches over children who never grow old and who seem to the bystander who knows their story 'like images' or like 'the rabbits on the grass.' It is as though Nature spoke through him at all times in the mood that is upon her when she is opening the apple-blossom or reddening the apple or thickening the shadow of the boughs, and that the men and women of his verse and of his stories are all the ministers of her mood.

IV

WHEN I WAS A CHILD I often heard my elders talking of an old turreted house where an old great-uncle of mine lived, and of its gardens and its long pond where there was an island with tame eagles; and one day somebody read me some verses and said they made him think of that old house where he had been very happy. The verses ran in my head for years and became to me the best description of happiness in the world, and I am not certain that I know a better even now. They were those first dozen verses of *Golden Wings* that begin—

> *'Midways of a walled garden*
> *In the happy poplar land*
> *Did an ancient castle stand,*
> *With an old knight for a warden.*

> *Many scarlet bricks there were*
> *In its walls, and old grey stone;*
> *Over which red apples shone*
> *At the right time of the year.*

> *On the bricks the green moss grew,*
> *Yellow lichen on the stone,*
> *Over which red apples shone;*
> *Little war that castle knew.'*

When William Morris describes a house of any kind, and makes his description poetical, it is always, I think, some house that he would have liked to have lived in, and I remember him saying about the time when he was writing of that great house of the Wolfings, 'I decorate modern houses for people, but the house that would please me would be some great room where one talked to one's friends in one corner and eat in another and slept in another and worked in another.' Indeed all he writes seems to me like the make-believe of a child who is remaking the world, not always in the same way, but always after its own heart; and so unlike all other modern writers he makes his poetry out of unending pictures of a happiness that is often what a child might imagine, and always a happiness that sets mind and body at ease. Now it is a picture of some great room full of merriment, now of the wine-press, now of the golden threshing-floor, now of an old mill among apple-trees, now of cool water after the heat of the sun, now of some well-sheltered, well-tilled place among woods or mountains, where men and women live happily, knowing of nothing that is too far off or too great for the affections. He has but one story to tell us, how some man or woman lost and found again the happiness that is always half of the body; and even when they are wandering from it, leaves must fall over them, and flowers make fragrances about them, and warm winds fan them, and birds sing to them, for being of Habundia's kin they must not forget the shadow of her Green Tree even for a moment, and the waters of her Well must be always wet upon their sandals. His poetry often wearies us as the unbroken green of July wearies us, for there is something in us, some bitterness because of the Fall it may be, that takes a little from the sweetness of Eve's apple after the first mouthful; but he who did all things gladly and easily, who never knew the curse of labour, found it always as sweet as it was in Eve's mouth. All kinds of associations have gathered about the pleasant things of the world and half taken the pleasure out of them for the greater number of men, but he saw them as when they came from the Divine Hand. I often see him in my mind as I saw him once at Hammersmith holding up a glass of claret towards the light and saying, 'Why do people say it is prosaic to get inspiration out of wine? Is it not the sunlight and the sap in the leaves? Are not grapes made by the sunlight and the sap?'

V

IN ONE OF HIS LITTLE socialist pamphlets he tells how he sat under an elm-tree and watched the starlings and thought of an old horse and an old labourer that had passed him by, and of the men and women he had seen in towns; and he wondered how all these had come to be as they were. He saw that the starlings were beautiful and merry and that men and the old horse they had subdued to their service were ugly and miserable, and yet the starlings, he thought, were of one kind whether there or in the south of England, and the ugly men and women were of one kind with those whose nobility and beauty had moved the ancient sculptors and poets to imagine the gods and the heroes after the images of men. Then he began, he tells us, to meditate how this great difference might be ended and a new life, which would permit men to have beauty in common among them as the starlings have, be built on the wrecks of the old life. In other words, his mind was illuminated from within and lifted into prophecy in the full right sense of the word, and he saw the natural things he was alone gifted to see in their perfect form; and having that faith which is alone worth having, for it includes all others, a sure knowledge established in the constitution of his mind that perfect things are final things, he announced that all he had seen would come to pass. I do not think he troubled to understand books of economics, and Mr. Mackail says, I think, that they vexed him and wearied him. He found it enough to hold up, as it were, life as it is to-day beside his visions, and to show how faded its colours were and how sapless it was. And if we had not enough artistic feeling, enough feeling for the perfect that is, to admit the authority of the vision; or enough faith to understand that all that is imperfect passes away, he would not, as I think, have argued with us in a serious spirit. Though I think that he never used the kinds of words I use in writing of him, though I think he would even have disliked a word like faith with its theological associations, I am certain that he understood thoroughly, as all artists understand a little, that the important things, the things we must believe in or perish, are beyond argument. We can no more reason about them than can the pigeon, come but lately from the egg, about the hawk whose shadow makes it cower among the grass. His vision is true because it is poetical, because we are a little happier when we are looking at it; and he knew as Shelley knew by an act of faith that the economists should take their measurements not from life as it is, but from the vision of men like him, from the vision of the world made perfect that is buried under all minds. The early Christians were of the kin of the Wilderness and of the Dry Tree, and they saw an unearthly Paradise, but he was of the kin of the Well and of the Green Tree and he saw an Earthly Paradise.

He obeyed his vision when he tried to make first his own house, for he was in this matter also like a child playing with the world, and then houses of other people, places where one could live happily; and he obeyed it when he wrote essays about the nature of happy work, and when he spoke at street corners about the coming changes.

He knew clearly what he was doing towards the end, for he lived at a time when poets and artists have begun again to carry the burdens that priests and theologians took from them angrily some few hundred years ago. His art was not more essentially religious than Rossetti's art, but it was different, for Rossetti, drunken with natural beauty, saw the supernatural beauty, the impossible beauty, in his frenzy, while he being less intense and more tranquil would show us a beauty that would wither if it did not set us at peace with natural things, and if we did not believe that it existed always a little, and would some day exist in its fulness. He may not have been, indeed he was not, among the very greatest of the poets, but he was among the greatest of those who prepare the last reconciliation when the Cross shall blossom with roses.

1902

THE PHILOSOPHY OF SHELLEY'S POETRY

I. His Ruling Ideas

WHEN I WAS A BOY in Dublin I was one of a group who rented a room in a mean street to discuss philosophy. My fellow-students got more and more interested in certain modern schools of mystical belief, and I never found anybody to share my one unshakable belief. I thought that whatever of philosophy has been made poetry is alone permanent, and that one should begin to arrange it in some regular order, rejecting nothing as the make-believe of the poets. I thought, so far as I can recollect my thoughts after so many years, that if a powerful and benevolent spirit has shaped the destiny of this world, we can better discover that destiny from the words that have gathered up the heart's desire of the world, than from historical records, or from speculation, wherein the heart withers. Since then I have observed dreams and visions very carefully, and am now certain that the imagination has some way of lighting on the truth that the reason has not, and that its commandments, delivered when the body is still and the reason silent, are the most binding we can ever know. I have re-read *Prometheus Unbound*, which I had hoped my fellow-students would have studied as a sacred book, and it seems to me to have an even more certain place than I had thought, among the sacred books of the world. I remember going to a learned scholar to ask about its deep meanings, which I felt more than understood, and his telling me that it was Godwin's *Political Justice* put into rhyme, and that Shelley was a crude revolutionist, and believed that the overturning of kings and priests would regenerate mankind. I quoted the lines which tell how the halcyons ceased to prey on fish, and how poisonous leaves became good for food, to show that he foresaw more than any political regeneration, but was too timid to push the argument. I still believe that one cannot help believing him, as this scholar I know believes him, a vague thinker, who mixed occasional great poetry with a phantastic rhetoric, unless one compares such passages, and above all such passages as describe the liberty he praised, till one has discovered the system of belief that lay behind them. It should seem natural to find his thought full of subtlety, for Mrs. Shelley has told how he hesitated whether he should be a metaphysician or a poet, and has spoken of his 'huntings after the obscure' with regret, and said of that *Prometheus Unbound*, which so many for three generations have thought *Political Justice* put into rhyme, 'It requires a mind as subtle and penetrating as his own to understand the mystic meanings scattered throughout the poem. They elude the ordinary reader by their abstraction and delicacy of distinction, but they are far from vague. It was his design to write prose metaphysical essays on the Nature of Man, which would have served to explain much of what is obscure in his poetry; a few scattered fragments of observation and remarks alone remain. He considered these philosophical views of mind and nature to be instinct with the intensest spirit of poetry.' From these scattered fragments and observations, and from many passages read in their light, one soon comes to understand that his liberty was so much more than the liberty of *Political Justice* that it was one with Intellectual Beauty, and that the regeneration he foresaw was so much more than the regeneration many political dreamers have foreseen, that it could not come in its perfection till the hours bore 'Time to his grave in eternity.' In *A Defence of Poetry*, the profoundest essay on the foundation of poetry in English, he shows that the poet and the lawgiver hold their station by the right of the same faculty, the one uttering in words and the other in the forms of society, his vision of the divine order, the Intellectual Beauty. 'Poets, according to the circumstances of the age and nation in which they appeared, were called in the earliest epoch of the world legislators or prophets, and a poet essentially comprises and unites both these characters. For he not only beholds intensely the present as it is, and discovers those laws according to which present things are to be ordained, but he beholds the future in the present, and his thoughts are the germs of the flowers and the fruit of latest time.' 'Language, colour, form, and religious and civil habits of action, are all the instruments and materials of poetry.' Poetry is 'the creation of actions according to the unchangeable process of human nature as existing in the mind of the creator, which is itself the image of all other minds.' 'Poets have been challenged to resign the civic crown to reasoners and merchants. . . It is admitted that the exercise of the imagination is the most delightful, but it is alleged that that of reason is the more useful. . . Whilst the mechanist abridges and the political economist combines labour, let them be sure that their speculations, for want of correspondence with those first principles which belong to the imagination, do not tend, as they have in modern England, to exasperate at once the extremes of luxury and want. . . The rich have become richer, the poor have become poorer, . . . such are the effects which must ever flow from an unmitigated exercise of the calculating faculty.' The speaker of these things might almost be Blake, who held that the Reason not only created Ugliness, but all other evils. The books of all wisdom are hidden in the cave of the Witch of Atlas, who is one of his personifications of beauty, and when she moves over the enchanted river that is an image of all life, the priests cast aside their deceits, and the king crowns an ape to mock his own sovereignty, and the soldiers gather about the anvils to beat their swords to ploughshares, and lovers cast away their timidity, and friends are united; while the power, which in *Laon and Cythna*, awakens the mind of the reformer to contend, and itself contends, against the tyrannies of the world, is first seen, as the star of love or beauty. And at the end of *The Ode to Naples*, he cries out to 'the spirit of beauty' to overturn the tyrannies of the world, or to fill them with its 'harmonizing ardours.' He calls the spirit of beauty liberty, because despotism, and perhaps, as 'the man of virtuous soul commands not nor obeys,' all authority, pluck virtue from her path towards beauty, and because it leads us by that love whose service is perfect freedom. It leads all things by love, for he cries again and again that love is the perception of beauty in thought and things, and it orders all things by love, for it is love that impels the soul to its expressions in thought and in action, by making us 'seek to awaken in all things that are, a community with what we experience within ourselves.' 'We are born into the world, and there is something within us which, from the instant that we live, more and more thirsts after its likeness.' We have 'a soul within our soul that describes a circle around its proper paradise which pain and sorrow and evil dare not overleap,' and we labour to see this soul in many mirrors, that we may possess it the more abundantly. He would hardly seek the progress of the world by any less gentle labour, and would hardly have us resist evil itself. He bids the reformers in *The Philosophical Review of Reform* receive 'the onset of the cavalry,' if it be sent to disperse their meetings, 'with folded arms,' and 'not because active resistance is not justifiable, but because temperance and courage would produce greater advantages than the most decisive victory;' and he gives them like advice in *The Masque of Anarchy*, for liberty, the poem cries, 'is love,' and can make the rich man kiss its feet, and, like those who followed Christ, give away his goods and follow it throughout the world.

He does not believe that the reformation of society can bring this beauty, this divine order, among men without the regeneration of the hearts of men. Even in *Queen Mab*, which was written before he had found his deepest thought, or rather perhaps before he had found words to utter it, for I do not think men change much in their deepest thought, he is less anxious to change men's beliefs, as I think, than to cry out against that serpent more subtle than any beast of the field, 'the cause and the effect of tyranny.' He affirms again and again that the virtuous, those who have 'pure desire and universal love,' are happy in the midst of tyranny, and he foresees a day when 'the spirit of nature,' the spirit of beauty of his later poems, who has her 'throne of power unappealable in every human heart,' shall have made men so virtuous that 'kingly glare will lose its power to dazzle and silently pass by,' and as it seems even commerce, 'the venal interchange of all that human art or nature yields, which wealth should purchase not,' come as silently to an end.

He was always, indeed in chief, a witness for that 'power unappealable.' Maddalo, in *Julian and Maddalo*, says that the soul is powerless, and can only, like a 'dreary bell hung in a heaven-illumined tower, toll our thoughts and our desires to meet round the rent heart and pray'; but Julian, who is Shelley himself, replies, as the makers of all religions have replied—

> *'Where is the beauty, love and truth we seek*
> *But in our minds? And if we were not weak,*
> *Should we be less in deed than in desire?'*

while *Mont Blanc* is an intricate analogy to affirm that the soul has its sources in 'the secret strength of things,' 'which governs thought and to the infinite heavens is a law.' He even thought that men might be immortal were they sinless, and his Cythna bids the sailors be without remorse, for all that live are stained as they are. It is thus, she says, that time marks men and their thoughts for the tomb. And the 'Red Comet,' the image of evil in *Laon and Cythna*, when it began its war with the star of beauty, brought not only 'Fear, Hatred, Fraud, and Tyranny,' but 'Death, Decay, Earthquake, and Blight and Madness pale.'

When the Red Comet is conquered, when Jupiter is overthrown by Demogorgon, when the prophecy of Queen Mab is fulfilled, visible nature will put on perfection again. He declares, in one of the notes to *Queen Mab*, that 'there is no great extravagance in presuming. . . that there should be a perfect identity between the moral and physical improvement of the human species,' and thinks it 'certain that wisdom is not compatible with disease, and that, in the present state of the climates of the earth, health in the true and comprehensive sense of the word is out of the reach of civilized man.' In *Prometheus Unbound* he sees, as in the ecstasy of a saint, the ships moving among the seas of the world without fear of danger

> *'by the light*
> *Of wave-reflected flowers, and floating odours,*
> *And music soft,'*

and poison dying out of the green things, and cruelty out of all living things, and even the toads and efts becoming beautiful, and at last Time being borne 'to his tomb in eternity.'

This beauty, this divine order, whereof all things shall become a part in a kind of resurrection of the body, is already visible to the dead and to souls in ecstasy, for ecstasy is a kind of death. The dying Lionel hears the song of the nightingale, and cries—

> *'Heardst thou not sweet words among*
> *That heaven-resounding minstrelsy?*
> *Heardst thou not that those who die*
> *Awake in a world of ecstasy?*
> *How love, when limbs are interwoven,*
> *And sleep, when the night of life is cloven,*
> *And thought to the world's dim boundaries clinging,*
> *And music when one beloved is singing,*
> *Is death? Let us drain right joyously*
> *The cup which the sweet bird fills for me.'*

And in the most famous passage in all his poetry he sings of Death as of a mistress. 'Life, like a dome of many-coloured glass, stains the white radiance of eternity.' 'Die, if thou wouldst be with that which thou wouldst seek;' and he sees his own soon-coming death in a rapture of prophecy, for 'the fire for which all thirst' beams upon him, 'consuming the last clouds of cold mortality.' When he is dead he will still influence the living, for though Adonais has fled 'to the burning fountains whence he came,' and 'is a portion of the eternal which must glow through time and change unquenchably the same,' and has 'awaked from the dream of life,' he has not gone from 'the young dawn,' or the 'caverns in the forests,' or 'the faint flowers and the fountains.' He has been 'made one with nature,' and his voice is 'heard in all her music,' and his presence is felt wherever 'that power may move which has withdrawn his being to its own,' and he bears 'his part' when it is compelling mortal things to their appointed forms, and he overshadows men's minds at their supreme moments, for

> *'when lofty thought*
> *Lifts a young heart above its mortal lair,*
> *And love and life contend in it for what*
> *Shall be its earthly doom, the dead live there,*
> *And move like winds of light on dark and stormy air.'*

'Of his speculations as to what will befall this inestimable spirit when we appear to die,' Mrs. Shelley has written, 'a mystic ideality tinged these speculations in Shelley's mind; certain stanzas in the poem of *The Sensitive Plant* express, in some degree, the almost inexpressible idea, not that we die into another state, when this state is no longer, from some reason, unapparent as well as apparent, accordant with our being—but that those who rise above the ordinary nature of man, fade from before our imperfect organs; they remain in their "love, beauty, and delight," in a world congenial to them, and we, clogged by "error, ignorance, and strife," see them not till we are fitted by purification and improvement to their higher state.' Not merely happy souls, but all beautiful places and movements and gestures and events, when we think they have ceased to be, have become portions of the eternal.

> *'In this life*
> *Of error, ignorance, and strife,*
> *Where nothing is, but all things seem,*
> *And we the shadows of the dream,*
>
> *It is a modest creed, and yet*
> *Pleasant, if one considers it,*
> *To own that death itself must be,*
> *Like all the rest, a mockery.*
>
> *This garden sweet, that lady fair,*
> *And all sweet shapes and odours there,*
> *In truth have never passed away;*
> *'Tis we, 'tis ours are changed, not they.*

> *For love and beauty and delight*
> *There is no death, nor change; their might*
> *Exceeds our organs, which endure*
> *No light, being themselves obscure.'*

He seems in his speculations to have lit on that memory of nature the visionaries claim for the foundation of their knowledge; but I do not know whether he thought, as they do, that all things good and evil remain for ever, 'thinking the thought and doing the deed,' though not, it may be, self-conscious; or only thought that 'love and beauty and delight' remain for ever. The passage where Queen Mab awakes 'all knowledge of the past,' and the good and evil 'events of old and wondrous times,' was no more doubtless than a part of the machinery of the poem, but all the machineries of poetry are parts of the convictions of antiquity, and readily become again convictions in minds that dwell upon them in a spirit of intense idealism.

Intellectual Beauty has not only the happy dead to do her will, but ministering spirits who correspond to the Devas of the East, and the Elemental Spirits of mediæval Europe, and the Sidhe of ancient Ireland, and whose too constant presence, and perhaps Shelley's ignorance of their more traditional forms, give some of his poetry an air of rootless phantasy. They change continually in his poetry, as they do in the visions of the mystics everywhere and of the common people in Ireland, and the forms of these changes display, in an especial sense, the glowing forms of his mind when freed from all impulse not out of itself or out of supersensual power. These are 'gleams of a remoter world which visit us in sleep,' spiritual essences whose shadows are the delights of all the senses, sounds 'folded in cells of crystal silence,' 'visions swift and sweet and quaint,' which lie waiting their moment 'each in his thin sheath like a chrysalis,' 'odours' among 'ever-blooming eden trees', 'liquors' that can give 'happy sleep,' or can make tears 'all wonder and delight'; 'The golden genii who spoke to the poets of Greece in dreams'; 'the phantoms' which become the forms of the arts when 'the mind, arising bright from the embrace of beauty,' 'casts on them the gathered rays which are reality'; the 'guardians' who move in 'the atmosphere of human thought' as 'the birds within the wind, or the fish within the wave,' or man's thought itself through all things; and who join the throng of the happy hours when Time is passing away—

> *'As the flying fish leap*
> *From the Indian deep,*
> *And mix with the seabirds half asleep.'*

It is these powers which lead Asia and Panthea, as they would lead all the affections of humanity, by words written upon leaves, by faint songs, by eddies of echoes that draw 'all spirits on that secret way,' by the 'dying odours' of flowers and by 'the sunlight of the sphered dew,' beyond the gates of birth and death to awake Demogorgon, eternity, that 'the painted veil' 'called life' may be 'torn aside.'

There are also ministers of ugliness and all evil, like those that came to Prometheus—

> *'As from the rose which the pale priestess kneels*
> *To gather for her festal crown of flowers,*
> *The aërial crimson falls, flushing her cheek,*
> *So from our victim's destined agony*
> *The shade which is our form invests us round;*
> *Else we are shapeless as our mother Night.'*

Or like those whose shapes the poet sees in *The Triumph of Life*, coming from the procession that follows the car of life, as 'hope' changes to 'desire,' shadows 'numerous as the dead leaves blown in autumn evening from a poplar tree'; and resembling those they come from, until, if I understand an obscure phrase aright, they are 'wrapt' round 'all the busy phantoms that live there as the sun shapes the clouds.' Some to sit 'chattering like apes,' and some like 'old anatomies' 'hatching their bare broods under the shade of dæmons' wings,' laughing 'to reassume the delegated powers' they had given to the tyrants of the earth, and some 'like small gnats and flies' to throng 'about the brow of lawyers, statesmen, priest and theorist,' and some 'like discoloured shapes of snow' to fall 'on fairest bosoms and the sunniest hair,' to be 'melted by the youthful glow which they extinguish,' and many to 'fling shadows of shadows yet unlike themselves,' shadows that are shaped into new forms by that 'creative ray' in which all move like motes.

These ministers of beauty and ugliness were certainly more than metaphors or picturesque phrases to one who believed the 'thoughts which are called real or external objects' differed but in regularity of recurrence from 'hallucinations, dreams, and the ideas of madness,' and lessened this difference by telling how he had dreamed 'three several times, between intervals of two or more years, the same precise dream,' and who had seen images with the mind's eye that left his nerves shaken for days together. Shadows that were as when there

> '*hovers*
> *A flock of vampire bats before the glare*
> *Of the tropic sun, bringing, ere evening,*
> *Strange night upon some Indian vale,*'

could not but have had more than a metaphorical and picturesque being to one who had spoken in terror with an image of himself, and who had fainted at the apparition of a woman with eyes in her breasts, and who had tried to burn down a wood, if we can trust Mrs. Williams' account, because he believed a devil, who had first tried to kill him, had sought refuge there.

It seems to me, indeed, that Shelley had reawakened in himself the age of faith, though there were times when he would doubt, as even the saints have doubted, and that he was a revolutionist, because he had heard the commandment, 'If ye know these things, happy are ye if ye do them.' I have re-read his *Prometheus Unbound* for the first time for many years, in the woods of Drim-da-rod, among the Echte hills, and sometimes I have looked towards Slieve-nan-Orr, where the country people say the last battle of the world shall be fought till the third day, when a priest shall lift a chalice, and the thousand years of peace begin. And I think this mysterious song utters a faith as simple and as ancient as the faith of those country people, in a form suited to a new age, that will understand, with Blake, that the holy spirit is 'an intellectual fountain,' and that the kinds and degrees of beauty are the images of its authority.

II. His Ruling Symbols

AT A COMPARATIVELY EARLY TIME Shelley made his imprisoned Cythna become wise in all human wisdom through the contemplation of her own mind, and write out this wisdom upon the sand in 'signs' that were 'clear elemental shapes whose smallest change' made 'a subtler language within language' and were 'the key of truths, which once were dimly taught in old Crotona.' His early romances and much throughout his poetry show how strong a fascination the traditions of magic and of the magical philosophy had cast over his mind, and one can hardly suppose that he had not brooded over their doctrine of symbols or signatures, though I do not find anything to show that he gave it any deep study. One finds in his poetry, besides innumerable images that have not the definiteness of symbols, many images that are certainly symbols, and as the years went by he began to use these with a more and more deliberately symbolic purpose. I imagine that, when he wrote his earlier poems, he allowed the subconscious life to lay its hands so firmly upon the rudder of his imagination, that he was little conscious of the abstract meaning of the images that rose in what seemed the idleness of his mind. Any one who has any experience of any mystical state of the soul knows how there float up in the mind profound symbols, whose meaning, if indeed they do not delude one into the dream that they are meaningless, one does not perhaps understand for years. Nor I think has any one, who has known that experience with any constancy, failed to find some day in some old book or on some old monument, a strange or intricate image, that had floated up before him, and grow perhaps dizzy with the sudden conviction that our little memories are but a part of some great memory that renews the world and men's thoughts age after age, and that our thoughts are not, as we suppose, the deep but a little foam upon the deep. Shelley understood this, as is proved by what he says of the eternity of beautiful things and of the influence of the dead, but whether he understood that the great memory is also a dwelling-house of symbols, of images that are living souls, I cannot tell. He had certainly experience of all but the most profound of the mystical states, of that union with created things which assuredly must precede the soul's union with the uncreated spirit. He says in his fragment of an essay upon life, mistaking a unique experience for the common experience of all: 'Let us recollect our sensations as children. . . we less habitually distinguished all that we saw and felt from ourselves. They seemed as it were to constitute one mass. There are some persons who in this respect are always children. Those who are subject to the state called reverie, feel as if their nature were resolved into the surrounding universe, or as if the surrounding universe were resolved into their being,' and he must have expected to receive thoughts and images from beyond his own mind, just in so far as that mind transcended its preoccupation with particular time and place, for he believed inspiration a kind of death; and he could hardly have helped perceiving that an image that has transcended particular time and place becomes a symbol, passes beyond death, as it were, and becomes a living soul.

When Shelley went to the Continent with Godwin's daughter in 1812 they sailed down certain great rivers in an open boat, and when he summed up in his preface to *Laon and Cythna* the things that helped to make him a poet, he spoke of these voyages: 'I have sailed down mighty rivers and seen the sun rise and set and the stars come forth whilst I sailed night and day down a rapid stream among mountains.'

He may have seen some cave that was the bed of a rivulet by some river side, or have followed some mountain stream to its source in a cave, for from his return to England rivers and streams and wells, flowing through caves or rising in them, came into every poem of his that was of any length, and always with the precision of symbols. Alastor passed in his boat along a river in a cave; and when for the last time he felt the presence of the spirit he loved and followed, it was when he watched his image in a silent well; and when he died it was where a river fell into 'an abysmal chasm'; and the Witch of Atlas in her gladness, as he in his sadness, passed in her boat along a river in a cave, and it was where it bubbled out of a cave that she was born; and when Rousseau, the typical poet of *The Triumph of Life*, awoke to the vision that was life, it was where a rivulet bubbled out of a cave; and the poet of *Epipsychidion* met the evil beauty 'by a well under blue nightshade bowers'; and Cythna bore her child imprisoned in a great cave beside 'a fountain round and vast and in which the wave imprisoned leaped and boiled perpetually'; and her lover Laon was brought to his prison in a high column through a cave where there was 'a putrid pool,' and when he went to see the conquered city he dismounted beside a polluted fountain in the market-place, foreshadowing thereby that spirit who at the end of *Prometheus Unbound* gazes at a regenerated city from 'within a fountain in the public square'; and when Laon and Cythna are dead they awake beside a fountain and drift into Paradise along a river; and at the end of things Prometheus and Asia are to live amid a happy world in a cave where a fountain 'leaps with an awakening sound'; and it was by a fountain, the meeting-place of certain unhappy lovers, that Rosalind and Helen told their unhappiness to one another; and it was under a willow by a fountain that the enchantress and her lover began their unhappy love; while his lesser poems and his prose fragments use caves and rivers and wells and fountains continually as metaphors. It may be that his subconscious life seized upon some passing scene, and moulded it into an ancient symbol without help from anything but that great memory; but so good a Platonist as Shelley could hardly have thought of any cave as a symbol,

WILLIAM BUTLER YEATS

without thinking of Plato's cave that was the world; and so good a scholar may well have had Porphyry on 'the Cave of the Nymphs' in his mind. When I compare Porphyry's description of the cave where the Phæacian boat left Odysseus, with Shelley's description of the cave of the Witch of Atlas, to name but one of many, I find it hard to think otherwise. I quote Taylor's translation, only putting Mr. Lang's prose for Taylor's bad verse. 'What does Homer obscurely signify by the cave in Ithaca which he describes in the following verses? "Now at the harbour's head is a long-leaved olive tree, and hard by is a pleasant cave and shadowy, sacred to the nymphs, that are called Naiads. And therein are mixing bowls and jars of stone, and there moreover do bees hive. And there are great looms of stone, whereon the nymphs weave raiment of purple stain, a marvel to behold; and there are waters welling ever more. Two gates there are to the cave, the one set towards the North wind, whereby men may go down, but the portals toward the South pertain rather to the gods, whereby men may not enter: it is the way of the immortals."' He goes on to argue that the cave was a temple before Homer wrote, and that 'the ancients did not establish temples without fabulous symbols,' and then begins to interpret Homer's description in all its detail. The ancients, he says, 'consecrated a cave to the world' and held 'the flowing waters' and the 'obscurity of the cavern' 'apt symbols of what the world contains,' and he calls to witness Zoroaster's cave with fountains; and often caves are, he says, symbols of 'all invisible power; because as caves are obscure and dark, so the essence of all these powers is occult,' and quotes a lost hymn to Apollo to prove that nymphs living in caves fed men 'from intellectual fountains'; and he contends that fountains and rivers symbolize generation, and that the word nymph 'is commonly applied to all souls descending into generation,' and that the two gates of Homer's cave are the gate of generation and the gate of ascent through death to the gods, the gate of cold and moisture, and the gate of heat and fire. Cold, he says, causes life in the world, and heat causes life among the gods, and the constellation of the cup is set in the heavens near the sign Cancer, because it is there that the souls descending from the Milky Way receive their draught of the intoxicating cold drink of generation. 'The mixing bowls and jars of stone' are consecrated to the Naiads, and are also, as it seems, symbolical of Bacchus, and are of stone because of the rocky beds of the rivers. And 'the looms of stone' are the symbols of the 'souls that descend into generation.' 'For the formation of the flesh is on or about the bones, which in the bodies of animals resemble stones,' and also because 'the body is a garment' not only about the soul, but about all essences that become visible, for 'the heavens are called by the ancients a veil, in consequence of being as it were the vestments of the celestial gods.' The bees hive in the mixing bowls and jars of stone, for so Porphyry understands the passage, because honey was the symbol adopted by the ancients for 'pleasure arising from generation.' The ancients, he says, called souls not only Naiads but bees, 'as the efficient cause of sweetness'; but not all souls 'proceeding into generation' are called bees, 'but those who will live in it justly and who after having performed such things as are acceptable to the gods will again return (to their kindred stars). For this insect loves to return to the place from whence it came and is eminently just and sober.' I find all these details in the cave of the Witch of Atlas, the most elaborately described of Shelley's caves, except the two gates, and these have a far-off echo in her summer journeys on her cavern river and in her winter sleep in 'an inextinguishable well of crimson fire.' We have for the mixing bowls, and jars of stone full of honey, those delights of the senses, 'sounds of air' 'folded in cells of crystal silences,' 'liquors clear and sweet' 'in crystal vials,' and for the bees, visions 'each in his thin sheath like a chrysalis,' and for 'the looms of stone' and 'raiment of purple stain' the Witch's spinning and embroidering; and the Witch herself is a Naiad, and was born from one of the Atlantides, who lay in 'a chamber of grey rock' until she was changed by the sun's embrace into a cloud.

When one turns to Shelley for an explanation of the cave and fountain one finds how close his thought was to Porphyry's. He looked upon thought as a condition of life in generation and believed that the reality beyond was something other than thought. He wrote in his fragment 'On Life,' 'That the basis of all things cannot be, as the popular philosophy alleges, mind, is sufficiently evident. Mind, as far as we have any experience of its properties, and beyond that experience how vain is argument, cannot create, it can only perceive;' and in another passage he defines mind as existence. Water is his great symbol of existence, and he continually meditates over its mysterious source. In his prose he tells how 'thought can with difficulty visit the intricate and winding chambers which it inhabits. It is like a river, whose rapid and perpetual stream flows outward. . . The caverns of the mind are obscure and shadowy; or pervaded with a lustre, beautiful and bright indeed, but shining not beyond their portals.' When the Witch has passed in her boat from the caverned river, that is doubtless her own destiny, she passes along the Nile 'by Moeris and the Mareotid lakes,' and sees all human life shadowed upon its waters in shadows that 'never are erased but tremble ever'; and in many a dark and subterranean street under the Nile—new caverns—and along the bank of the Nile; and as she bends over the unhappy, she compares unhappiness to 'the strife that stirs the liquid surface of man's life'; and because she can see the reality of things she is described as journeying 'in the calm depths' of 'the wide lake' we journey over unpiloted. Alastor calls the river that he follows an image of his mind, and thinks that it will be as hard to say where his thought will be when he is dead as where its waters will be in ocean or cloud in a little while. In *Mont Blanc*, a poem so overladen with descriptions in parentheses that one loses sight of its logic, Shelley compares the flowing through our mind of 'the universe of things,' which are, he has explained elsewhere, but thoughts, to the flowing of the Arne through the ravine, and compares the unknown sources of our thoughts in some 'remoter world' whose 'gleams' 'visit the soul in sleep,' to Arne's sources among the glaciers on the mountain heights. Cythna in the passage where she speaks of making signs 'a subtle language within language' on the sand by the 'fountain' of sea water in the cave where she is imprisoned, speaks of the 'cave' of her mind which gave its secrets to her, and of 'one mind the type of all' which is a 'moveless wave' reflecting 'all moveless things that are'; and then passing more completely under the power of the symbol, she speaks of growing wise through contemplation of the images that rise out of the fountain at the call of her will. Again and again one finds some passing allusion to the cave of man's mind, or to the caves of his youth, or to the cave of mysteries we enter at death, for to Shelley as to Porphyry it is more than an image of life in the world. It may mean any enclosed life, as when it is the dwelling-place of Asia and Prometheus, or when it is 'the still cave of poetry,' and it may have all meanings at once, or it may have as little meaning as some ancient religious symbol enwoven from the habit of centuries with the patterns of a carpet or a tapestry.

As Shelley sailed along those great rivers and saw or imagined the cave that associated itself with rivers in his mind, he saw half-ruined towers upon the hilltops, and once at any rate a tower is used to symbolize a meaning that is the contrary to the meaning symbolized by caves. Cythna's lover is brought through the cave where there is a polluted fountain to a high tower, for being man's far-seeing mind, when the world has cast him out he must to the 'towers of thought's crowned powers';

nor is it possible for Shelley to have forgotten this first imprisonment when he made men imprison Lionel in a tower for a like offence; and because I know how hard it is to forget a symbolical meaning, once one has found it, I believe Shelley had more than a romantic scene in his mind when he made Prince Athanase follow his mysterious studies in a lighted tower above the sea, and when he made the old hermit watch over Laon in his sickness in a half-ruined tower, wherein the sea, here doubtless as to Cythna, 'the one mind,' threw 'spangled sands' and 'rarest sea shells.' The tower, important in Maeterlinck, as in Shelley, is, like the sea, and rivers, and caves with fountains, a very ancient symbol, and would perhaps, as years went by, have grown more important in his poetry. The contrast between it and the cave in *Laon and Cythna* suggests a contrast between the mind looking outward upon men and things and the mind looking inward upon itself, which may or may not have been in Shelley's mind, but certainly helps, with one knows not how many other dim meanings, to give the poem mystery and shadow. It is only by ancient symbols, by symbols that have numberless meanings beside the one or two the writer lays an emphasis upon, or the half-score he knows of, that any highly subjective art can escape from the barrenness and shallowness of a too conscious arrangement, into the abundance and depth of nature. The poet of essences and pure ideas must seek in the half-lights that glimmer from symbol to symbol as if to the ends of the earth, all that the epic and dramatic poet finds of mystery and shadow in the accidental circumstance of life.

The most important, the most precise of all Shelley's symbols, the one he uses with the fullest knowledge of its meaning, is the Morning and Evening Star. It rises and sets for ever over the towers and rivers, and is the throne of his genius. Personified as a woman it leads Rousseau, the typical poet of *The Triumph of Life*, under the power of the destroying hunger of life, under the power of the sun that we shall find presently as a symbol of life, and it is the Morning Star that wars against the principle of evil in *Laon and Cythna*, at first as a star with a red comet, here a symbol of all evil as it is of disorder in *Epipsychidion*, and then as a serpent with an eagle—symbols in Blake too and in the Alchemists; and it is the Morning Star that appears as a winged youth to a woman, who typifies humanity amid its sorrows, in the first canto of *Laon and Cythna*; and it is evoked by the wailing women of *Hellas*, who call it 'lamp of the free' and 'beacon of love' and would go where it hides flying from the deepening night among those 'kingless continents sinless as Eden,' and 'mountains and islands' 'prankt on the sapphire sea' that are but the opposing hemispheres to the senses but, as I think, the ideal world, the world of the dead, to the imagination; and in the *Ode to Liberty*, Liberty is bid lead wisdom out of the inmost cave of man's mind as the Morning Star leads the sun out of the waves. We know too that had *Prince Athanase* been finished it would have described the finding of Pandemus, the stars' lower genius, and the growing weary of her, and the coming to its true genius Urania at the coming of death, as the day finds the Star at evening. There is hardly indeed a poem of any length in which one does not find it as a symbol of love, or liberty, or wisdom, or beauty, or of some other expression of that Intellectual Beauty, which was to Shelley's mind the central power of the world; and to its faint and fleeting light he offers up all desires, that are as

> *'The desire of the Moth for the star,*
> *The desire for something afar*
> *From the sphere of our sorrow.'*

When its genius comes to Rousseau, shedding dew with one hand, and treading out the stars with her feet, for she is also the genius of the dawn, she brings him a cup full of oblivion and love. He drinks and his mind becomes like sand 'on desert Labrador' marked by the feet of deer and a wolf. And then the new vision, life, the cold light of day moves before him, and the first vision becomes an invisible presence. The same image was in his mind too when he wrote

> *'Hesperus flies from awakening night*
> *And pants in its beauty with speed and light,*
> *Fast fleeting, soft and bright.'*

Though I do not think that Shelley needed to go to Porphyry's account of the cold intoxicating cup, given to the souls in the constellation of the Cup near the constellation Cancer, for so obvious a symbol as the cup, or that he could not have found the wolf and the deer and the continual flight of his Star in his own mind, his poetry becomes the richer, the more emotional, and loses something of its appearance of idle phantasy when I remember that these are ancient symbols, and still come to visionaries in their dreams. Because the wolf is but a more violent symbol of longing and desire than the hound, his wolf and deer remind me of the hound and deer that Usheen saw in the Gaelic poem chasing one another on the water before he saw the young man following the woman with the golden apple; and of a Galway tale that tells how Niam, whose name means brightness or beauty, came to Usheen as a deer; and of a vision that a friend of mine saw when gazing at a dark-blue curtain. I was with a number of Hermetists, and one of them said to another, 'Do you see something in the curtain?' The other gazed at the curtain for a while and saw presently a man led through a wood by a black hound, and then the hound lay dead at a place the seer knew was called, without knowing why, 'the Meeting of the Suns,' and the man followed a red hound, and then the red hound was pierced by a spear. A white fawn watched the man out of the wood, but he did not look at it, for a white hound came and he followed it trembling, but the seer knew that he would follow the fawn at last, and that it would lead him among the gods. The most learned of the Hermetists said, 'I cannot tell the meaning of the hounds or where the Meeting of the Suns is, but I think the fawn is the Morning and Evening Star.' I have little doubt that when the man saw the white fawn he was coming out of the darkness and passion of the world into some day of partial regeneration, and that it was the Morning Star and would be the Evening Star at its second coming. I have little doubt that it was but the story of Prince Athanase and what may have been the story of Rousseau in *The Triumph of Life*, thrown outward once again from that great memory, which is still the mother of the Muses, though men no longer believe in it.

It may have been this memory, or it may have been some impulse of his nature too subtle for his mind to follow, that made Keats, with his love of embodied things, of precision of form and colouring, of emotions made sleepy by the flesh, see Intellectual Beauty in the Moon; and Blake, who lived in that energy he called eternal delight, see it in the Sun, where his personification of poetic genius labours at a furnace. I think there was certainly some reason why these men took so deep a pleasure in lights, that Shelley thought of with weariness and trouble. The Moon is the most changeable of symbols, and not merely because it is the symbol of change. As mistress of the waters she governs the life of instinct and the generation of things, for as Porphyry says, even 'the apparition of images' in the 'imagination' is through 'an excess of moisture'; and, as a cold and changeable fire set in the bare heavens, she governs alike chastity and the joyless idle drifting hither and thither of generated things. She may give God a body and have Gabriel to bear her messages, or she may come to men in their happy moments as she came to Endymion, or she may deny life and shoot her arrows; but because she only becomes beautiful in giving herself, and is no flying ideal, she is not loved by the children of desire.

Shelley could not help but see her with unfriendly eyes. He is believed to have described Mary Shelley at a time when she had come to seem cold in his eyes, in that passage of *Epipsychidion* which tells how a woman like the Moon led him to her cave and made 'frost' creep over the sea of his mind, and so bewitched life and death with 'her silver voice' that they ran from him crying, 'Away, he is not of our crew.' When he describes the Moon as part of some beautiful scene he can call her beautiful, but when he personifies, when his words come under the influence of that great memory or of some mysterious tide in the depth of our being, he grows unfriendly or not truly friendly or at the most pitiful. The Moon's lips 'are pale and waning,' it is 'the cold Moon,' or 'the frozen and inconstant Moon,' or it is 'forgotten' and 'waning,' or it 'wanders' and is 'weary,' or it is 'pale and grey,' or it is 'pale for weariness,' and 'wandering companionless' and 'ever changing,' and finding 'no object worth' its 'constancy,' or it is like a 'dying lady' who 'totters' 'out of her chamber led by the insane and feeble wanderings of her fading brain,' and even when it is no more than a star, it casts an evil influence that makes the lips of lovers 'lurid' or pale. It only becomes a thing of delight when Time is being borne to his tomb in eternity, for then the spirit of the Earth, man's procreant mind, fills it with his own joyousness. He describes the spirit of the Earth and of the Moon, moving above the rivulet of their lives in a passage which reads like a half-understood vision. Man has become 'one harmonious soul of many a soul' and 'all things flow to all' and 'familiar acts are beautiful through love,' and an 'animation of delight' at this change flows from spirit to spirit till the snow 'is loosened from the Moon's lifeless mountains.'

Some old magical writer, I forget who, says if you wish to be melancholy hold in your left hand an image of the Moon made out of silver, and if you wish to be happy hold in your right hand an image of the Sun made out of gold. The Sun is the symbol of sensitive life, and of belief and joy and pride and energy, of indeed the whole life of the will, and of that beauty which neither lures from far off, nor becomes beautiful in giving itself, but makes all glad because it is beauty. Taylor quotes Proclus as calling it 'the Demiurgos of everything sensible.' It was therefore natural that Blake, who was always praising energy, and all exalted overflowing of oneself, and who thought art an impassioned labour to keep men from doubt and despondency, and woman's love an evil, when it would trammel the man's will, should see the poetic genius not in a woman star but in the Sun, and should rejoice throughout his poetry in 'the Sun in his strength.' Shelley, however, except when he uses it to describe the peculiar beauty of Emilia Viviani, who was 'like an incarnation of the Sun when light is changed to love,' saw it with less friendly eyes. He seems to have seen it with perfect happiness only when veiled in mist, or glimmering upon water, or when faint enough to do no more than veil the brightness of his own Star; and in *The Triumph of Life*, the one poem in which it is part of the avowed symbolism, its power is the being and the source of all tyrannies. When the woman personifying the Morning Star has faded from before his eyes, Rousseau sees a 'new vision' in 'a cold bright car' with a rainbow hovering over her, and as she comes the shadow passes from 'leaf and stone,' and the souls she has enslaved seem in 'that light like atomies to dance within a sunbeam,' or they dance among the flowers that grow up newly 'in the grassy verdure of the desert,' unmindful of the misery that is to come upon them. 'These are the great, the unforgotten,' all who have worn 'mitres and helms and crowns or wreaths of light,' and yet have not known themselves. Even 'great Plato' is there because he knew joy and sorrow, because life that could not subdue him by gold or pain, by 'age or sloth or slavery,' subdued him by love. All who have ever lived are there except Christ and Socrates and 'the sacred few' who put away all life could give, being doubtless followers throughout their lives of the forms borne by the flying ideal, or who, 'as soon as they had touched the world with living flame, flew back like eagles to their native noon.'

In ancient times, it seems to me that Blake, who for all his protest was glad to be alive, and ever spoke of his gladness, would have worshipped in some chapel of the Sun, and that Keats, who accepted life gladly though 'with a delicious diligent indolence,' would have worshipped in some chapel of the Moon, but that Shelley, who hated life because he sought 'more in life than any understood,' would have wandered, lost in a ceaseless reverie, in some chapel of the Star of infinite desire.

I think too that as he knelt before an altar, where a thin flame burnt in a lamp made of green agate, a single vision would have come to him again and again, a vision of a boat drifting down a broad river between high hills where there were caves and towers, and following the light of one Star; and that voices would have told him how there is for every man some one scene, some one adventure, some one picture that is the image of his secret life, for wisdom first speaks in images, and that this one image, if he would but brood over it his life long, would lead his soul, disentangled from unmeaning circumstance and the ebb and flow of the world, into that far household, where the undying gods await all whose souls have become simple as flame, whose bodies have become quiet as an agate lamp.

But he was born in a day when the old wisdom had vanished and was content merely to write verses, and often with little thought of more than verses.

1900

At Stratford-On-Avon

I

I HAVE BEEN HEARING SHAKESPEARE, as the traveller in *News from Nowhere* might have heard him, had he not been hurried back into our noisy time. One passes through quiet streets, where gabled and red-tiled houses remember the Middle Age, to a theatre that has been made not to make money, but for the pleasure of making it, like the market houses that set the traveller chuckling; nor does one find it among hurrying cabs and ringing pavements, but in a green garden by a river side. Inside I have to be content for a while with a chair, for I am unexpected, and there is not an empty seat but this; and yet there is no one who has come merely because one must go somewhere after dinner. All day, too, one does not hear or see an incongruous or noisy thing, but spends the hours reading the plays, and the wise and foolish things men have said of them, in the library of the theatre, with its oak-panelled walls and leaded windows of tinted glass; or one rows by reedy banks and by old farmhouses, and by old churches among great trees. It is certainly one's fault if one opens a newspaper, for Mr. Benson gives one a new play every night, and one need talk of nothing but the play in the inn-parlour, under the oak beams blackened by time and showing the mark of the adze that shaped them. I have seen this week *King John*, *Richard II*, the second part of *Henry IV*, *Henry V*, the second part of *Henry VI*, and *Richard III* played in their right order, with all the links that bind play to play unbroken; and partly because of a spirit in the place, and partly because of the way play supports play, the theatre has moved me as it has never done before. That strange procession of kings and queens, of warring nobles, of insurgent crowds, of courtiers, and of people of the gutter has been to me almost too visible, too audible, too full of an unearthly energy. I have felt as I have sometimes felt on grey days on the Galway shore, when a faint mist has hung over the grey sea and the grey stones, as if the world might suddenly vanish and leave nothing behind, not even a little dust under one's feet. The people my mind's eye has seen have too much of the extravagance of dreams, like all the inventions of art before our crowded life had brought moderation and compromise, to seem more than a dream, and yet all else has grown dim before them.

In London the first man one meets puts any high dream out of one's head, for he will talk to one of something at once vapid and exciting, some one of those many subjects of thought that build up our social unity. But here he gives back one's dream like a mirror. If we do not talk of the plays, we talk of the theatre, and how more people may be got to come, and our isolation from common things makes the future become grandiose and important. One man tells how the theatre and the library were at their foundation but part of a scheme the future is to fulfil. To them will be added a school where speech, and gesture, and fencing, and all else that an actor needs will be taught, and the council, which will have enlarged its Festivals to some six weeks, will engage all the chief players of Shakespeare, and perhaps of other great dramatists in this and other countries. These chief players will need to bring but few of their supporters, for the school will be able to fill all the lesser parts with players who are slowly recovering the lost tradition of musical speech. Another man is certain that the Festival, even without the school, which would require a new endowment, will grow in importance year by year, and that it may become with favouring chance the supreme dramatic event of the world; and when I suggest that it may help to break the evil prestige of London he becomes enthusiastic.

Surely a bitter hatred of London is becoming a mark of those that love the arts, and all that have this hatred should help anything that looks like a beginning of a centre of art elsewhere. The easiness of travel, which is always growing, began by emptying the country, but it may end by filling it; for adventures like this of Stratford-on-Avon show that people are ready to journey from all parts of England and Scotland and Ireland, and even from America, to live with their favourite art as shut away from the world as though they were 'in retreat,' as Catholics say. Nobody but an impressionist painter, who hides it in light and mist, even pretends to love a street for its own sake; and could we meet our friends and hear music and poetry in the country, none of us that are not captive would ever leave the thrushes. In London, we hear something that we like some twice or thrice in a winter, and among people who are thinking the while of a music-hall singer or of a member of parliament, but there we would hear it and see it among people who liked it well enough to have travelled some few hours to find it; and because those who care for the arts have few near friendships among those that do not, we would hear and see it among near friends. We would escape, too, from those artificial tastes and interests we cultivate, that we may have something to talk about among people we meet for a few minutes and not again, and the arts would grow serious as the Ten Commandments.

II

I DO NOT THINK THERE is anything I disliked in Stratford, beside certain new houses, but the shape of the theatre; and as a larger theatre must be built sooner or later, that would be no great matter if one could put a wiser shape into somebody's head. I cannot think there is any excuse for a half-round theatre, where land is not expensive, or no very great audience to be seated within earshot of the stage; or that it was adopted for a better reason than because it has come down to us, though from a time when the art of the stage was a different art. The Elizabethan theatre was a half-round, because the players were content to speak their lines on a platform, as if they were speakers at a public meeting, and we go on building in the same shape, although our art of the stage is the art of making a succession of pictures. Were our theatres of the shape of a half-closed fan, like Wagner's theatre, where the audience sit on seats that rise towards the broad end while the play is played at the narrow end, their pictures could be composed for eyes at a small number of points of view, instead of for eyes at many points of view, above and below and at the sides, and what is no better than a trade might become an art. With the eyes watching from the sides of a half-round, on the floor and in the boxes and galleries, would go the solid-built houses and the flat trees that shake with every breath of air; and we could make our pictures with robes that contrasted with great masses of colour in the back cloth and such severe or decorative forms of hills and trees and houses as would not overwhelm, as our naturalistic scenery does, the idealistic art of the poet, and all at a little price. Naturalistic scene-painting is not an art, but a trade, because it is, at best, an attempt to copy the more obvious effects of nature by the methods of the ordinary landscape-painter, and by his methods made coarse and summary. It is but flashy landscape-painting and lowers the taste it appeals to, for the taste it appeals to has been formed by a more delicate art. Decorative scene-painting would be, on the other hand, as inseparable from the movements as from the robes of the players and from the falling of the light; and being in itself a grave and quiet thing it would mingle with the tones of the voices and with the sentiment of the play, without overwhelming them under an alien interest. It would be a new and legitimate art appealing to a taste formed by itself and copying nothing but itself. Mr. Gordon Craig used scenery of this kind at the Purcell Society performance the other day, and despite some marring of his effects by the half-round shape of the theatre, it was the first beautiful scenery our stage has seen. He created an ideal country where everything was possible, even speaking in verse, or speaking in music, or the expression of the whole of life in a dance, and I would like to see Stratford-on-Avon decorate its Shakespeare with like scenery. As we cannot, it seems, go back to the platform and the curtain, and the argument for doing so is not without weight, we can only get rid of the sense of unreality, which most of us feel when we listen to the conventional speech of Shakespeare, by making scenery as conventional. Time after time his people use at some moment of deep emotion an elaborate or deliberate metaphor, or do some improbable thing which breaks an emotion of reality we have imposed upon him by an art that is not his, nor in the spirit of his. It also is an essential part of his method to give slight or obscure motives of many actions that our attention may dwell on what is of chief importance, and we set these cloudy actions among solid-looking houses, and what we hope are solid-looking trees, and illusion comes to an end, slain by our desire to increase it. In his art, as in all the older art of the world, there was much make-believe, and our scenery, too, should remember the time when, as my nurse used to tell me, herons built their nests in old men's beards! Mr. Benson did not venture to play the scene in *Richard III* where the ghosts walk, as Shakespeare wrote it, but had his scenery been as simple as Mr. Gordon Craig's purple back cloth that made Dido and Æneas seem wandering on the edge of eternity, he would have found nothing absurd in pitching the tents of Richard and Richmond side by side. Goethe has said, 'Art is art, because it is not nature!' It brings us near to the archetypal ideas themselves, and away from nature, which is but their looking-glass.

III

In *La Peau de Chagrin* Balzac spends many pages in describing a coquette, who seems the image of heartlessness, and then invents an improbable incident that her chief victim may discover how beautifully she can sing. Nobody had ever heard her sing, and yet in her singing, and in her chatter with her maid, Balzac tells us, was her true self. He would have us understand that behind the momentary self, which acts and lives in the world, and is subject to the judgment of the world, there is that which cannot be called before any mortal Judgment seat, even though a great poet, or novelist, or philosopher be sitting upon it. Great literature has always been written in a like spirit, and is, indeed, the Forgiveness of Sin, and when we find it becoming the Accusation of Sin, as in George Eliot, who plucks her Tito in pieces with as much assurance as if he had been clockwork, literature has begun to change into something else. George Eliot had a fierceness one hardly finds but in a woman turned argumentative, but the habit of mind her fierceness gave its life to was characteristic of her century, and is the habit of mind of the Shakespearian critics. They and she grew up in a century of utilitarianism, when nothing about a man seemed important except his utility to the State, and nothing so useful to the State as the actions whose effect can be weighed by the reason. The deeds of Coriolanus, Hamlet, Timon, Richard II had no obvious use, were, indeed, no more than the expression of their personalities, and so it was thought Shakespeare was accusing them, and telling us to be careful lest we deserve the like accusations. It did not occur to the critics that you cannot know a man from his actions, because you cannot watch him in every kind of circumstance, and that men are made useless to the State as often by abundance as by emptiness, and that a man's business may at times be revelation, and not reformation. Fortinbras was, it is likely enough, a better King than Hamlet would have been, Aufidius was a more reasonable man than Coriolanus, Henry V was a better man-at-arms than Richard II, but after all, were not those others who changed nothing for the better and many things for the worse greater in the Divine Hierarchies? Blake has said that 'the roaring of lions, the howling of wolves, the raging of the stormy sea, and the destructive sword are portions of Eternity, too great for the eye of man,' but Blake belonged by right to the ages of Faith, and thought the State of less moment than the Divine Hierarchies. Because reason can only discover completely the use of those obvious actions which everybody admires, and because every character was to be judged by efficiency in action, Shakespearian criticism became a vulgar worshipper of Success. I have turned over many books in the library at Stratford-on-Avon, and I have found in nearly all an antithesis, which grew in clearness and violence as the century grew older, between two types, whose representatives were Richard II, 'sentimental,' 'weak,' 'selfish,' 'insincere,' and Henry V, 'Shakespeare's only hero.' These books took the same delight in abasing Richard II that school-boys do in persecuting some boy of fine temperament, who has weak muscles and a distaste for school games. And they had the admiration for Henry V that school-boys have for the sailor or soldier hero of a romance in some boys' paper. I cannot claim any minute knowledge of these books, but I think that these emotions began among the German critics, who perhaps saw something French and Latin in Richard II, and I know that Professor Dowden, whose book I once read carefully, first made these emotions eloquent and plausible. He lived in Ireland, where everything has failed, and he meditated frequently upon the perfection of character which had, he thought, made England successful, for, as we say, 'cows beyond the water have long horns.' He forgot that England, as Gordon has said, was made by her adventurers, by her people of wildness and imagination and eccentricity; and thought that Henry V, who only seemed to be these things because he had some commonplace vices, was not only the typical Anglo-Saxon, but the model Shakespeare held up before England; and he even thought it worth while pointing out that Shakespeare himself was making a large fortune while he was writing about Henry's victories. In Professor Dowden's successors this apotheosis went further; and it reached its height at a moment of imperialistic enthusiasm, of ever-deepening conviction that the commonplace shall inherit the earth, when somebody of reputation, whose name I cannot remember, wrote that Shakespeare admired this one character alone out of all his characters. The Accusation of Sin produced its necessary fruit, hatred of all that was abundant, extravagant, exuberant, of all that sets a sail for shipwreck, and flattery of the commonplace emotions and conventional ideals of the mob, the chief Paymaster of accusation.

IV

I cannot believe that Shakespeare looked on his Richard II with any but sympathetic eyes, understanding indeed how ill-fitted he was to be King, at a certain moment of history, but understanding that he was lovable and full of capricious fancy, 'a wild creature' as Pater has called him. The man on whom Shakespeare modelled him had been full of French elegancies, as he knew from Hollingshead, and had given life a new luxury, a new splendour, and been 'too friendly' to his friends, 'too favourable' to his enemies. And certainly Shakespeare had these things in his head when he made his King fail, a little because he lacked some qualities that were doubtless common among his scullions, but more because he had certain qualities that are uncommon in all ages. To suppose that Shakespeare preferred the men who deposed his King is to suppose that Shakespeare judged men with the eyes of a Municipal Councillor weighing the merits of a Town Clerk; and that had he been by when Verlaine cried out from his bed, 'Sir, you have been made by the stroke of a pen, but I have been made by the breath of God,' he would have thought the Hospital Superintendent the better man. He saw indeed, as I think, in Richard II the defeat that awaits all, whether they be Artist or Saint, who find themselves where men ask of them a rough energy and have nothing to give but some contemplative virtue, whether lyrical phantasy, or sweetness of temper, or dreamy dignity, or love of God, or love of His creatures. He saw that such a man through sheer bewilderment and impatience can become as unjust or as violent as any common man, any Bolingbroke or Prince John, and yet remain 'that sweet lovely rose.' The courtly and saintly ideals of the Middle Ages were fading, and the practical ideals of the modern age had begun to threaten the unuseful dome of the sky; Merry England was fading, and yet it was not so faded that the Poets could not watch the procession of the world with that untroubled sympathy for men as they are, as apart from all they do and seem, which is the substance of tragic irony.

Shakespeare cared little for the State, the source of all our judgments, apart from its shows and splendours, its turmoils and battles, its flamings out of the uncivilized heart. He did indeed think it wrong to overturn a King, and thereby to swamp peace in civil war, and the historical plays from *Henry IV* to *Richard III*, that monstrous birth and last sign of the wrath of Heaven, are a fulfilment of the prophecy of the Bishop of Carlisle, who was 'raised up by God' to make it; but he had no nice sense of utilities, no ready balance to measure deeds, like that fine instrument, with all the latest improvements, Gervinus and Professor Dowden handle so skilfully. He meditated as Solomon, not as Bentham meditated, upon blind ambitions, untoward accidents, and capricious passions, and the world was almost as empty in his eyes as it must be in the eyes of God.

> *'Tired with all these, for restful death I cry;—*
> *As, to behold desert a beggar born,*
> *And needy nothing trimm'd in jollity,*
> *And purest faith unhappily forsworn,*
> *And gilded honour shamefully misplaced,*
> *And maiden virtue rudely strumpeted,*

And right perfection wrongfully disgrac'd,
And strength by limping sway disabled,
And Art made tongue-tied by authority,
And folly, doctor-like, controlling skill,
And simple truth miscalled simplicity,
And captive good attending captain ill:
Tired with all these, from these would I begone
Save that, to die, I leave my love alone.'

V

THE GREEKS, A CERTAIN SCHOLAR has told me, considered that myths are the activities of the Dæmons, and that the Dæmons shape our characters and our lives. I have often had the fancy that there is some one Myth for every man, which, if we but knew it, would make us understand all he did and thought. Shakespeare's Myth, it may be, describes a wise man who was blind from very wisdom, and an empty man who thrust him from his place, and saw all that could be seen from very emptiness. It is in the story of Hamlet, who saw too great issues everywhere to play the trivial game of life, and of Fortinbras, who came from fighting battles about 'a little patch of ground' so poor that one of his Captains would not give 'six ducats' to 'farm it,' and who was yet acclaimed by Hamlet and by all as the only befitting King. And it is in the story of Richard II, that unripened Hamlet, and of Henry V, that ripened Fortinbras. To poise character against character was an element in Shakespeare's art, and scarcely a play is lacking in characters that are the complement of one another, and so, having made the vessel of porcelain Richard II, he had to make the vessel of clay Henry V He makes him the reverse of all that Richard was. He has the gross vices, the coarse nerves, of one who is to rule among violent people, and he is so little 'too friendly' to his friends that he bundles them out of doors when their time is over. He is as remorseless and undistinguished as some natural force, and the finest thing in his play is the way his old companions fall out of it broken-hearted or on their way to the gallows; and instead of that lyricism which rose out of Richard's mind like the jet of a fountain to fall again where it had risen, instead of that phantasy too enfolded in its own sincerity to make any thought the hour had need of, Shakespeare has given him a resounding rhetoric that moves men, as a leading article does to-day. His purposes are so intelligible to everybody that everybody talks of him as if he succeeded, although he fails in the end, as all men great and little fail in Shakespeare, and yet his conquests abroad are made nothing by a woman turned warrior, and that boy he and Katherine were to 'compound,' 'half French, half English,' 'that' was to 'go to Constantinople and take the Turk by the beard,' turns out a Saint, and loses all his father had built up at home and his own life.

Shakespeare watched Henry V not indeed as he watched the greater souls in the visionary procession, but cheerfully, as one watches some handsome spirited horse, and he spoke his tale, as he spoke all tales, with tragic irony.

VI

THE FIVE PLAYS, THAT ARE but one play, have, when played one after another, something extravagant and superhuman, something almost mythological. Those nobles with their indifference to death and their immense energy seem at times no nearer the common stature of men than do the Gods and the heroes of Greek plays. Had there been no Renaissance and no Italian influence to bring in the stories of other lands English history would, it may be, have become as important to the English imagination as the Greek Myths to the Greek imagination; and many plays by many poets would have woven it into a single story whose contours, vast as those of Greek myth, would have made living men and women seem like swallows building their nests under the architrave of some Temple of the Giants. English literature, because it would have grown out of itself, might have had the simplicity and unity of Greek literature, for I can never get out of my head that no man, even though he be Shakespeare, can write perfectly when his web is woven of threads that have been spun in many lands. And yet, could those foreign tales have come in if the great famine, the sinking down of popular imagination, the dying out of traditional phantasy, the ebbing out of the energy of race, had not made them necessary? The metaphors and language of Euphuism, compounded of the natural history and mythology of the classics, were doubtless a necessity also, that something might be poured into the emptiness. Yet how they injured the simplicity and unity of the speech! Shakespeare wrote at a time when solitary great men were gathering to themselves the fire that had once flowed hither and thither among all men, when individualism in work and thought and emotion was breaking up the old rhythms of life, when the common people, no longer uplifted by the myths of Christianity and of still older faiths, were sinking into the earth.

The people of Stratford-on-Avon have remembered little about him, and invented no legend to his glory. They have remembered a drinking-bout of his, and invented some bad verses for him, and that is about all. Had he been some hard-drinking, hard-living, hard-riding, loud-blaspheming Squire they would have enlarged his fame by a legend of his dealings with the devil; but in his day the glory of a Poet, like that of all other imaginative powers, had ceased, or almost ceased outside a narrow class. The poor Gaelic rhymer leaves a nobler memory among his neighbours, who will talk of Angels standing like flames about his death-bed, and of voices speaking out of bramble-bushes that he may have the wisdom of the world. The Puritanism that drove the theatres into Surrey was but part of an inexplicable movement that was trampling out the minds of all but some few thousands born to cultivated ease.

May 1901

William Blake and the Imagination

There have been men who loved the future like a mistress, and the future mixed her breath into their breath and shook her hair about them, and hid them from the understanding of their times. William Blake was one of these men, and if he spoke confusedly and obscurely it was because he spoke things for whose speaking he could find no models in the world about him. He announced the religion of art, of which no man dreamed in the world about him; and he understood it more perfectly than the thousands of subtle spirits who have received its baptism in the world about us, because, in the beginning of important things—in the beginning of love, in the beginning of the day, in the beginning of any work, there is a moment when we understand more perfectly than we understand again until all is finished. In his time educated people believed that they amused themselves with books of imagination but that they 'made their souls' by listening to sermons and by doing or by not doing certain things. When they had to explain why serious people like themselves honoured the great poets greatly they were hard put to it for lack of good reasons. In our time we are agreed that we 'make our souls' out of some one of the great poets of ancient times, or out of Shelley or Wordsworth, or Goethe or Balzac, or Flaubert, or Count Tolstoy, in the books he wrote before he became a prophet and fell into a lesser order, or out of Mr. Whistler's pictures, while we amuse ourselves, or, at best, make a poorer sort of soul, by listening to sermons or by doing or by not doing certain things. We write of great writers, even of writers whose beauty would once have seemed an unholy beauty, with rapt sentences like those our fathers kept for the beatitudes and mysteries of the Church; and no matter what we believe with our lips, we believe with our hearts that beautiful things, as Browning said in his one prose essay that was not in verse, have 'lain burningly on the Divine hand,' and that when time has begun to wither, the Divine hand will fall heavily on bad taste and vulgarity. When no man believed these things William Blake believed them, and began that preaching against the Philistine, which is as the preaching of the Middle Ages against the Saracen.

He had learned from Jacob Boehme and from old alchemist writers that imagination was the first emanation of divinity, 'the body of God,' 'the Divine members,' and he drew the deduction, which they did not draw, that the imaginative arts were therefore the greatest of Divine revelations, and that the sympathy with all living things, sinful and righteous alike, which the imaginative arts awaken, is that forgiveness of sins commanded by Christ. The reason, and by the reason he meant deductions from the observations of the senses, binds us to mortality because it binds us to the senses, and divides us from each other by showing us our clashing interests; but imagination divides us from mortality by the immortality of beauty, and binds us to each other by opening the secret doors of all hearts. He cried again and again that every thing that lives is holy, and that nothing is unholy except things that do not live—lethargies, and cruelties, and timidities, and that denial of imagination which is the root they grew from in old times. Passions, because most living, are most holy—and this was a scandalous paradox in his time—and man shall enter eternity borne upon their wings.

And he understood this so literally that certain drawings to *Vala*, had he carried them beyond the first faint pencillings, the first faint washes of colour, would have been a pretty scandal to his time and to our time. The sensations of this 'foolish body,' this 'phantom of the earth and water,' were in themselves but half-living things, 'vegetative' things, but passion that 'eternal glory' made them a part of the body of God.

This philosophy kept him more simply a poet than any poet of his time, for it made him content to express every beautiful feeling that came into his head without troubling about its utility or chaining it to any utility. Sometimes one feels, even when one is reading poets of a better time— Tennyson or Wordsworth, let us say—that they have troubled the energy and simplicity of their imaginative passions by asking whether they were for the helping or for the hindrance of the world, instead of believing that all beautiful things have 'lain burningly on the Divine hand.' But when one reads Blake, it is as though the spray of an inexhaustible fountain of beauty was blown into our faces, and not merely when one reads the *Songs of Innocence*, or the lyrics he wished to call 'The Ideas of Good and Evil,' but when one reads those 'Prophetic Works' in which he spoke confusedly and obscurely because he spoke of things for whose speaking he could find no models in the world about him. He was a symbolist who had to invent his symbols; and his counties of England, with their correspondence to tribes of Israel, and his mountains and rivers, with their correspondence to parts of a man's body, are arbitrary as some of the symbolism in the *Axël* of the symbolist Villiers De L'Isle Adam is arbitrary, while they mix incongruous things as *Axël* does not. He was a man crying out for a mythology, and trying to make one because he could not find one to his hand. Had he been a Catholic of Dante's time he would have been well content with Mary and the angels; or had he been a scholar of our time he would have taken his symbols where Wagner took his, from Norse mythology; or have followed, with the help of Prof. Rhys, that pathway into Welsh mythology which he found in 'Jerusalem'; or have gone to Ireland—and he was probably an Irishman—and chosen for his symbols the sacred mountains, along whose sides the peasant still sees enchanted fires, and the divinities which have not faded from the belief, if they have faded from the prayers of simple hearts; and have spoken without mixing incongruous things because he spoke of things that had been long steeped in emotion; and have been less obscure because a traditional mythology stood on the threshold of his meaning and on the margin of his sacred darkness. If 'Enitharmon' had been named Freia, or Gwydeon, or Danu, and made live in Ancient Norway, or Ancient Wales, or Ancient Ireland, we would have forgotten that her maker was a mystic; and the hymn of her harping, that is in *Vala*, would but have reminded us of many ancient hymns.

> '*The joy of woman is the death of her beloved,*
> *Who dies for love of her,*
> *In torments of fierce jealousy and pangs of adoration.*
> *The lover's night bears on my song,*
> *And the nine spheres rejoice beneath my powerful control.*
>
> *They sing unwearied to the notes of my immortal hand.*
> *The solemn, silent moon*
> *Reverberates the long harmony sounding upon my limbs.*
> *The birds and beasts rejoice and play,*
> *And every one seeks for his mate to prove his inmost joy.*
>
> *Furious and terrible they rend the nether deep,*
> *The deep lifts up his rugged head,*
> *And lost in infinite hovering wings vanishes with a cry.*
> *The fading cry is ever dying,*
> *The living voice is ever living in its inmost joy.*'

1897

WILLIAM BUTLER YEATS

WILLIAM BLAKE AND HIS ILLUSTRATIONS
TO *THE DIVINE COMEDY*

I. His Opinions Upon Art

WILLIAM BLAKE WAS THE FIRST writer of modern times to preach the indissoluble marriage of all great art with symbol. There had been allegorists and teachers of allegory in plenty, but the symbolic imagination, or, as Blake preferred to call it, 'vision,' is not allegory, being 'a representation of what actually exists really and unchangeably.' A symbol is indeed the only possible expression of some invisible essence, a transparent lamp about a spiritual flame; while allegory is one of many possible representations of an embodied thing, or familiar principle, and belongs to fancy and not to imagination: the one is a revelation, the other an amusement. It is happily no part of my purpose to expound in detail the relations he believed to exist between symbol and mind, for in doing so I should come upon not a few doctrines which, though they have not been difficult to many simple persons, ascetics wrapped in skins, women who had cast away all common knowledge, peasants dreaming by their sheepfolds upon the hills, are full of obscurity to the man of modern culture; but it is necessary to just touch upon these relations, because in them was the fountain of much of the practice and of all the precept of his artistic life.

If a man would enter into 'Noah's rainbow,' he has written, and 'make a friend' of one of 'the images of wonder' which dwell there, and which always entreat him 'to leave mortal things,' 'then would he arise from the grave and meet the Lord in the air'; and by this rainbow, this sign of a covenant granted to him who is with Shem and Japhet, 'painting, poetry and music,' 'the three powers in man of conversing with Paradise which the flood "of time and space" did not sweep away,' Blake represented the shapes of beauty haunting our moments of inspiration: shapes held by most for the frailest of ephemera, but by him for a people older than the world, citizens of eternity, appearing and reappearing in the minds of artists and of poets, creating all we touch and see by casting distorted images of themselves upon 'the vegetable glass of nature'; and because beings, none the less symbols, blossoms, as it were, growing from invisible immortal roots, hands, as it were, pointing the way into some divine labyrinth. If 'the world of imagination' was 'the world of eternity,' as this doctrine implied, it was of less importance to know men and nature than to distinguish the beings and substances of imagination from those of a more perishable kind, created by the phantasy, in uninspired moments, out of memory and whim; and this could best be done by purifying one's mind, as with a flame, in study of the works of the great masters, who were great because they had been granted by divine favour a vision of the unfallen world from which others are kept apart by the flaming sword that turns every way; and by flying from the painters who studied 'the vegetable glass' for its own sake, and not to discover there the shadows of imperishable beings and substances, and who entered into their own minds, not to make the unfallen world a test of all they heard and saw and felt with the senses, but to cover the naked spirit with 'the rotten rags of memory' of older sensations. The struggle of the first part of his life had been to distinguish between these two schools, and to cleave always to the Florentine, and so to escape the fascination of those who seemed to him to offer the sleep of nature to a spirit weary with the labours of inspiration; but it was only after his return to London from Felpham in 1804 that he finally escaped from 'temptations and perturbations' which sought to destroy 'the imaginative power' at 'the hands of Venetian and Flemish Demons.' 'The spirit of Titian'—and one must always remember that he had only seen poor engravings, and what his disciple, Palmer, has called 'picture-dealers' Titians'—'was particularly active in raising doubts concerning the possibility of executing without a model; and when once he had raised the doubt it became easy for him to snatch away the vision time after time'; and Blake's imagination 'weakened' and 'darkened' until a 'memory of nature and of the pictures of various schools possessed his mind, instead of appropriate execution' flowing from the vision itself. But now he wrote, 'O glory, and O delight! I have entirely reduced that spectrous fiend to his station'—he had overcome the merely reasoning and sensual portion of the mind—'whose annoyance has been the ruin of my labours for the last twenty years of my life. . . I speak with perfect confidence and certainty of the fact which has passed upon me. Nebuchadnezzar had seven times passed over him, I have had twenty; thank God I was not altogether a beast as he was. . . Suddenly, on the day after visiting the Truchsessian Gallery of pictures'—this was a gallery containing pictures by Albert Dürer and by the great Florentines—'I was again enlightened with the light I enjoyed in my youth, and which had for exactly twenty years been closed from me, as by a door and window shutters. . . Excuse my enthusiasm, or rather madness, for I am really drunk with intellectual vision whenever I take a pencil or graver in my hand, as I used to be in my youth.'

This letter may have been the expression of a moment's enthusiasm, but was more probably rooted in one of those intuitions of coming technical power which every creator feels, and learns to rely upon; for all his greatest work was done, and the principles of his art were formulated, after this date. Except a word here and there, his writings hitherto had not dealt with the principles of art except remotely and by implication; but now he wrote much upon them, and not in obscure symbolic verse, but in emphatic prose, and explicit if not very poetical rhyme. In his *Descriptive Catalogue*, in *The Address to the Public*, in the notes on Sir Joshua Reynolds, in *The Book of Moonlight*—of which some not very dignified rhymes alone remain—in beautiful detached passages in *The Ms. Book*, he explained spiritual art, and praised the painters of Florence and their influence, and cursed all that has come of Venice and Holland. The limitation of his view was from the very intensity of his vision; he was a too literal realist of imagination, as others are of nature; and because he believed that the figures seen by the mind's eye, when exalted by inspiration, were 'eternal existences,' symbols of divine essences, he hated every grace of style that might obscure their lineaments. To wrap them about in reflected lights was to do this, and to dwell over-fondly upon any softness of hair or flesh was to dwell upon that which was least permanent and least characteristic, for 'The great and golden rule of art, as of life, is this: that the more distinct, sharp and wiry the boundary-line, the more perfect the work of art; and the less keen and sharp, the greater is the evidence of weak imitation, plagiarism and bungling.' Inspiration was to see the permanent and characteristic in all forms, and if you had it not, you must needs imitate with a languid mind the things you saw or remembered, and so sink into the sleep of nature where all is soft and melting. 'Great inventors in all ages knew this. Protogenes and Apelles knew each other by their line. Raphael and Michael Angelo and Albert Dürer are known by this and this alone. How do we distinguish the owl from the beast, the horse from the ox, but by the bounding outline? How do we distinguish one face or countenance from another but by the bounding-line and its infinite inflections and movements? What is it that builds a house and plants a garden but the definite and determinate? What is it that distinguished honesty from knavery but the hard and wiry line of rectitude and certainty in the actions and intentions? Leave out this line and you leave out life itself; and all is chaos again, and the line of the Almighty must be drawn out upon it before man or beast can exist.' He even insisted that 'colouring does not depend upon where the colours are put, but upon where the light and dark are put, and all depends upon the form or outline'—meaning, I suppose, that a colour gets its brilliance or its depth from being in light or in shadow. He does not mean by outline the bounding-line dividing a form from its background, as one of his commentators has thought, but the line that divides it from surrounding space, and unless you have an overmastering sense of this you cannot draw true beauty at all, but only 'the beauty that is appended to folly,' a beauty of mere voluptuous softness, 'a lamentable accident of the mortal and perishing life,' for 'the beauty proper for sublime art is lineaments, or forms and features capable of being the receptacles of intellect,' and 'the face or limbs that alter least from youth to old age are the face and limbs of the greatest beauty and perfection.' His praise of a severe art had been beyond price had his age rested a moment to listen, in the midst of its enthusiasm for Correggio and the later Renaissance, for Bartolozzi and for Stothard; and yet in his visionary realism, and in his enthusiasm for what, after all, is perhaps the greatest art, and a necessary part of every picture that is art at all, he forgot how he who wraps the vision in lights and shadows, in iridescent or glowing colour, having in the midst of his labour many little visions of these secondary essences, until form be half lost in pattern, may compel the canvas or paper to become itself a symbol of some not indefinite because unsearchable essence; for is not the Bacchus and Ariadne of Titian a talisman as powerfully charged with intellectual virtue as though it were a jewel-studded door of the city seen on Patmos?

To cover the imperishable lineaments of beauty with shadows and reflected lights was to fall into the power of his 'Vala,' the indolent fascination of nature, the woman divinity who is so often described in 'the prophetic books' as 'sweet pestilence,' and whose children weave webs to take the souls of men; but there was yet a more lamentable chance, for nature has also a 'masculine portion' or 'spectre' which kills instead of merely hiding, and is continually at war with inspiration. To 'generalize' forms and shadows, to 'smooth out' spaces and lines in obedience to 'laws of composition,' and of painting; founded, not upon imagination, which always thirsts for variety and delights in freedom, but upon reasoning from sensation which is always seeking to reduce everything to a lifeless and slavish uniformity; as the popular art of

Blake's day had done, and as he understood Sir Joshua Reynolds to advise, was to fall into 'Entuthon Benithon,' or 'the Lake of Udan Adan,' or some other of those regions where the imagination and the flesh are alike dead, that he names by so many resonant phantastical names. 'General knowledge is remote knowledge,' he wrote; 'it is in particulars that wisdom consists, and happiness too. Both in art and life general masses are as much art as a pasteboard man is human. Every man has eyes, nose and mouth; this every idiot knows. But he who enters into and discriminates most minutely the manners and intentions, the characters in all their branches, is the alone wise or sensible man, and on this discrimination all art is founded. . . As poetry admits not a letter that is insignificant, so painting admits not a grain of sand or a blade of grass insignificant, much less an insignificant blot or blur.'

Against another desire of his time, derivative also from what he has called 'corporeal reason,' the desire for a 'tepid moderation,' for a lifeless 'sanity in both art and life,' he had protested years before with a paradoxical violence. 'The roadway of excess leads to the palace of wisdom,' and we must only 'bring out weight and measure in time of dearth.' This protest, carried, in the notes on Sir Joshua Reynolds, to the point of dwelling with pleasure on the thought that 'The *Lives of the Painters* say that Raphael died of dissipation,' because dissipation is better than emotional penury, seemed as important to his old age as to his youth. He taught it to his disciples, and one finds it in its purely artistic shape in a diary written by Samuel Palmer, in 1824: 'Excess is the essential vivifying spirit, vital spark, embalming spice of the finest art. There are many mediums in the *means*—none, oh, not a jot, not a shadow of a jot, in the *end* of great art. In a picture whose merit is to be excessively brilliant, it can't be too brilliant, but individual tints may be too brilliant. . . We must not begin with medium, but think always on excess and only use medium to make excess more abundantly excessive.'

These three primary commands, to seek a determinate outline, to avoid a generalized treatment, and to desire always abundance and exuberance, were insisted upon with vehement anger, and their opponents called again and again 'demons' and 'villains,' 'hired' by the wealthy and the idle; but in private, Palmer has told us, he could find 'sources of delight throughout the whole range of art,' and was ever ready to praise excellence in any school, finding, doubtless, among friends, no need for the emphasis of exaggeration. There is a beautiful passage in 'Jerusalem' in which the merely mortal part of the mind, 'the spectre,' creates 'pyramids of pride,' and 'pillars in the deepest hell to reach the heavenly arches,' and seeks to discover wisdom in 'the spaces between the stars,' not 'in the stars,' where it is, but the immortal part makes all his labours vain, and turns his pyramids to 'grains of sand,' his 'pillars' to 'dust on the fly's wing,' and makes of 'his starry heavens a moth of gold and silver mocking his anxious grasp.' So when man's desire to rest from spiritual labour, and his thirst to fill his art with mere sensation and memory, seem upon the point of triumph, some miracle transforms them to a new inspiration; and here and there among the pictures born of sensation and memory is the murmuring of a new ritual, the glimmering of new talismans and symbols.

It was during and after the writing of these opinions that Blake did the various series of pictures which have brought him the bulk of his fame. He had already completed the illustrations to Young's *Night Thoughts*—in which the great sprawling figures, a little wearisome even with the luminous colours of the original water-colour, became nearly intolerable in plain black and white—and almost all the illustrations to 'the prophetic books,' which have an energy like that of the elements, but are rather rapid sketches taken while some phantasmic procession swept over him, than elaborate compositions, and in whose shadowy adventures one finds not merely, as did Dr. Garth Wilkinson, 'the hells of the ancient people, the Anakim, the Nephalim, and the Rephaim. . . gigantic petrifactions from which the fires of lust and intense selfish passion have long dissipated what was animal and vital'; not merely the shadows cast by the powers who had closed the light from him as 'with a door and window shutters,' but the shadows of those who gave them battle. He did now, however, the many designs to Milton, of which I have only seen those to *Paradise Regained*; the reproductions of those to *Comus*, published, I think, by Mr. Quaritch; and the three or four to *Paradise Lost*, engraved by Bell Scott—a series of designs which one good judge considers his greatest work; the illustrations to Blair's *Grave*, whose gravity and passion struggle with the mechanical softness and trivial smoothness of Schiavonetti's engraving; the illustrations to Thornton's *Virgil*, whose influence is manifest in the work of the little group of landscape-painters who gathered about him in his old age and delighted to call him master. The member of the group, whom I have already so often quoted, has alone praised worthily these illustrations to the first *eclogue*: 'There is in all such a misty and dreamy glimmer as penetrates and kindles the inmost soul and gives complete and unreserved delight, unlike the gaudy daylight of this world. They are like all this wonderful artist's work, the drawing aside of the fleshly curtain, and the glimpse which all the most holy, studious saints and sages have enjoyed, of the rest which remains to the people of God.' Now, too, he did the great series, the crowning work of his life, the illustrations to *The Book of Job* and the illustrations to *The Divine Comedy*. Hitherto he had protested against the mechanical 'dots and lozenges' and 'blots and blurs' of Woollett and Strange, but had himself used both 'dot and lozenge,' 'blot and blur,' though always in subordination 'to a firm and determinate outline'; but in Marc Antonio, certain of whose engravings he was shown by Linnell, he found a style full of delicate lines, a style where all was living and energetic, strong and subtle. And almost his last words, a letter written upon his death-bed, attack the 'dots and lozenges' with even more than usually quaint symbolism, and praise expressive lines. 'I know that the majority of Englishmen are bound by the indefinite. . . a line is a line in its minutest particulars, straight or crooked. It is itself not intermeasurable by anything else. . . but since the French Revolution'—since the reign of reason began, that is—'Englishmen are all intermeasurable with one another, certainly a happy state of agreement in which I do not agree.' The Dante series occupied the last years of his life; even when too weak to get out of bed he worked on, propped up with the great drawing-book before him. He sketched a hundred designs, but left all incomplete, some very greatly so, and partly engraved seven plates, of which the 'Francesca and Paolo' is the most finished. It is not, I think, inferior to any but the finest in the Job, if indeed to them, and shows in its perfection Blake's mastery over elemental things, the swirl in which the lost spirits are hurried, 'a watery flame' he would have called it, the haunted waters and the huddling shapes. In the illustrations of Purgatory there is a serene beauty, and one finds his Dante and Virgil climbing among the rough rocks under a cloudy sun, and in their sleep upon the smooth steps towards the summit, a placid, marmoreal, tender, starry rapture.

All in this great series are in some measure powerful and moving, and not, as it is customary to say of the work of Blake, because a flaming imagination pierces through a cloudy and indecisive technique, but because they have the only excellence possible in any art, a mastery over artistic expression. The technique of Blake was imperfect, incomplete, as is the technique of well-nigh all artists who have striven to bring fires from remote summits; but where his imagination is perfect and complete, his technique has a like perfection, a like completeness. He strove to embody more subtle raptures, more elaborate intuitions than any before him; his imagination and technique are more broken and strained under a great burden than the imagination and technique of any other master. 'I am,' wrote Blake, 'like others, just equal in invention and execution.' And again, 'No man can improve an original invention; nor can an original invention exist without execution, organized, delineated and articulated either by God or man. . . I have heard people say, "Give me the ideas; it is no matter what words you put them into;" and others say, "Give me the designs; it is no matter for the execution." . . . Ideas cannot be given but in their minutely appropriate words, nor can a design be made without its minutely appropriate execution.' Living in a time when technique and imagination are continually perfect and complete, because they no longer strive to bring fire from heaven, we forget how imperfect and incomplete they were in even the greatest masters, in Botticelli, in Orcagna, and in Giotto.

The errors in the handiwork of exalted spirits are as the more phantastical errors in their lives; as Coleridge's opium cloud; as Villiers De L'Isle Adam's candidature for the throne of Greece; as Blake's anger against causes and purposes he but half understood; as the flickering madness an Eastern scripture would allow in august dreamers; for he who half lives in eternity endures a rending of the structures of the mind, a crucifixion of the intellectual body.

II. His Opinions on Dante

As Blake sat bent over the great drawing-book, in which he made his designs to *The Divine Comedy*, he was very certain that he and Dante represented spiritual states which face one another in an eternal enmity. Dante, because a great poet, was 'inspired by the Holy Ghost'; but his inspiration was mingled with a certain philosophy, blown up out of his age, which Blake held for mortal and the enemy of immortal things, and which from the earliest times has sat in high places and ruled the world. This philosophy was the philosophy of soldiers, of men of the world, of priests busy with government, of all who, because of the absorption in active life, have been persuaded to judge and to punish, and partly also, he admitted, the philosophy of Christ, who in descending into the world had to take on the world; who, in being born of Mary, a symbol of the law in Blake's symbolic language, had to 'take after his mother,' and drive the money-changers out of the Temple. Opposed to this was another philosophy, not made by men of action, drudges of time and space, but by Christ when wrapped in the divine essence, and by artists and poets, who are taught by the nature of their craft to sympathize with all living things, and who, the more pure and fragrant is their lamp, pass the further from all limitations, to come at last to forget good and evil in an absorbing vision of the happy and the unhappy. The one philosophy was worldly, and established for the ordering of the body and the fallen will, and so long as it did not call its 'laws of prudence' 'the laws of God,' was a necessity, because 'you cannot have liberty in this world without what you call moral virtue'; the other was divine, and established for the peace of the imagination and the unfallen will, and, even when obeyed with a too literal reverence, could make men sin against no higher principality than prudence. He called the followers of the first philosophy pagans, no matter by what name they knew themselves, because the pagans, as he understood the word pagan, believed more in the outward life, and in what he called 'war, princedom, and victory,' than in the secret life of the spirit; and the followers of the second philosophy Christians, because only those whose sympathies had been enlarged and instructed by art and poetry could obey the Christian command of unlimited forgiveness. Blake had already found this 'pagan' philosophy in Swedenborg, in Milton, in Wordsworth, in Sir Joshua Reynolds, in many persons, and it had roused him so constantly and to such angry paradox that its overthrow became the signal passion of his life, and filled all he did and thought with the excitement of a supreme issue. Its kingdom was bound to grow weaker so soon as life began to lose a little in crude passion and naïve tumult, but Blake was the first to announce its successor, and he did this, as must needs be with revolutionists who have 'the law' for 'mother,' with a firm conviction that the things his opponents held white were indeed black, and that the things they held black, white; with a strong persuasion that all busy with government are men darkness and 'something other than human life'; one is reminded of Shelley, who was the next to take up the cry, though with a less abundant philosophic faculty, but still more of Nietzsche, whose thought flows always, though with an even more violent current, in the bed Blake's thought has worn.

The kingdom that was passing was, he held, the kingdom of the Tree of Knowledge; the kingdom that was coming was the kingdom of the Tree of Life: men who ate from the Tree of Knowledge wasted their days in anger against one another, and in taking one another captive in great nets; men who sought their food among the green leaves of the Tree of Life condemned none but the unimaginative and the idle, and those who forget that even love and death and old age are an imaginative art.

In these opposing kingdoms is the explanation of the petulant sayings he wrote on the margins of the great sketch-book, and of those others, still more petulant, which Crabb Robinson has recorded in his diary. The sayings about the forgiveness of sins have no need for further explanation, and are in contrast with the attitude of that excellent commentator, Herr Hettinger, who, though Dante swooned from pity at the tale of Francesca, will only 'sympathize' with her 'to a certain extent,' being taken in a theological net. 'It seems as if Dante,' Blake wrote, 'supposes God was something superior to the Father of Jesus; for if He gives rain to the evil and the good, and His sun to the just and the unjust, He can never have builded Dante's Hell, nor the Hell of the Bible, as our parsons explain it. It must have been framed by the dark spirit itself, and so I understand it.' And again, 'Whatever task is of vengeance and whatever is against forgiveness of sin is not of the Father but of Satan, the accuser, the father of Hell.' And again, and this time to Crabb Robinson, 'Dante saw devils where I saw none. I see good only.' 'I have never known a very bad man who had not something very good about him.' This forgiveness was not the forgiveness of the theologian who has received a commandment from afar off, but of the poet and artist, who believes he has been taught, in a mystical vision, 'that the imagination is the man himself,' and believes he has discovered in the practice of his art that without a perfect sympathy there is no perfect imagination, and therefore no perfect life. At another moment he called Dante 'an atheist, a mere politician busied about this world, as Milton was, till, in his old age, returned to God whom he had had in his childhood.' 'Everything is atheism,' he has already explained, 'which assumed the reality of the natural and unspiritual world.' Dante, he held, assumed its reality when he made obedience to its laws a condition of man's happiness hereafter, and he set Swedenborg beside Dante in misbelief for calling Nature 'the ultimate of Heaven,' a lowest rung, as it were, of Jacob's ladder, instead of a net woven by Satan to entangle our wandering joys and bring our hearts into captivity. There are certain curious unfinished diagrams scattered here and there among the now separated pages of the sketch-book, and of these there is one which, had it had all its concentric rings filled with names, would have been a systematic exposition of his animosities and of their various intensity. It represents Paradise, and in the midst, where Dante emerges from the earthly Paradise, is written 'Homer,' and in the next circle 'Swedenborg,' and on the margin these words: 'Everything in Dante's Paradise shows that he has made the earth the foundation of all, and its goddess Nature, memory,' memory of sensations, 'not the Holy Ghost. . . Round Purgatory is Paradise, and round Paradise vacuum. Homer is the centre of all, I mean the poetry of the heathen.' The statement that round Paradise is vacuum is a proof of the persistence of his ideas, and of his curiously literal understanding of his own symbols; for it is but another form of the charge made against Milton many years before in *The Marriage of Heaven and Hell*. 'In Milton the Father is destiny, the son a ratio of the five senses,' Blake's definition of the reason which is the enemy of the imagination, 'and the Holy Ghost vacuum.' Dante, like other medieval mystics, symbolized the highest order of created beings by the fixed stars, and God by the darkness beyond them, the *Primum Mobile*. Blake, absorbed in his very different vision, in which God took always a human shape, believed that to think of God under a symbol drawn from the outer world was in itself idolatry, but that to imagine Him as an unpeopled immensity was to think of Him under the one symbol furthest from His essence—it being a creation of the ruining reason, 'generalizing' away 'the minute particulars of life.' Instead of seeking God in the deserts of time and space, in exterior immensities, in what he called 'the abstract void,' he believed that the further he dropped behind him memory of time and space, reason built upon sensation, morality founded for the ordering of the world; and the more he was absorbed in emotion; and, above all, in emotion escaped from the impulse of bodily longing and the restraints of bodily reason, in artistic emotion; the nearer did he come to Eden's 'breathing garden,' to use his beautiful phrase, and to the unveiled face of God. No worthy symbol of God existed but the inner world, the true humanity, to whose various aspects he gave many names, 'Jerusalem,' 'Liberty,' 'Eden,' 'The Divine Vision,' 'The Body of God,' 'The Human Form Divine,' 'The Divine Members,' and whose most intimate expression was art and poetry. He always sang of God under this symbol:

> *'For Mercy, Pity, Peace, and Love*
> *Is God Our Father dear;*
> *And Mercy, Pity, Peace, and Love*
> *Is man, His child and care.*

For Mercy has a human heart;
Pity a human face;
And Love the human form divine;
And Peace, the human dress.

Then every man of every clime,
That prays in his distress,
Prays to the human form divine—
Love, Mercy, Pity, Peace.'

Whenever he gave this symbol a habitation in space he set it in the sun, the father of light and life; and set in the darkness beyond the stars, where light and life die away, Og and Anak and the giants that were of old, and the iron throne of Satan.

By thus contrasting Blake and Dante by the light of Blake's paradoxical wisdom, and as though there was no important truth hung from Dante's beam of the balance, I but seek to interpret a little-understood philosophy rather than one incorporate in the thought and habits of Christendom. Every philosophy has half its truth from times and generations; and to us one-half of the philosophy of Dante is less living than his poetry, while the truth Blake preached and sang and painted is the root of the cultivated life, of the fragile perfect blossom of the world born in ages of leisure and peace, and never yet to last more than a little season; the life those Phæacians, who told Odysseus that they had set their hearts in nothing but in 'the dance and changes of raiment, and love and sleep,' lived before Poseidon heaped a mountain above them; the lives of all who, having eaten of the Tree of Life, love, more than did the barbarous ages when none had time to live, 'the minute particulars of life,' the little fragments of space and time, which are wholly flooded by beautiful emotion because they are so little they are hardly of time and space at all. 'Every space smaller than a globule of man's blood,' he wrote, 'opens into eternity of which this vegetable earth is but a shadow.' And again, 'Every time less than a pulsation of the artery is equal' in its tenor and value 'to six thousand years, for in this period the poet's work is done, and all the great events of time start forth, and are conceived: in such a period, within a moment, a pulsation of the artery.' Dante, indeed, taught, in the 'Purgatorio,' that sin and virtue are alike from love, and that love is from God; but this love he would restrain by a complex eternal law, a complex external Church. Blake upon the other hand cried scorn upon the whole spectacle of external things, a vision to pass away in a moment, and preached the cultivated life, the internal Church which has no laws but beauty, rapture and labour. 'I know of no other Christianity, and of no other gospel, than the liberty, both of body and mind, to exercise the divine arts of imagination, the real and eternal world of which this vegetable universe is but a faint shadow, and in which we shall live in our eternal or imaginative bodies when these vegetable mortal bodies are no more. The Apostles knew of no other gospel. What are all their spiritual gifts? What is the divine spirit? Is the Holy Ghost any other than an intellectual fountain? What is the harvest of the gospel and its labours? What is the talent which it is a curse to hide? What are the treasures of heaven which we are to lay up for ourselves? Are they any other than mental studies and performances? What are all the gifts of the gospel, are they not all mental gifts? Is God a spirit who must be worshipped in spirit and truth? Are not the gifts of the spirit everything to man? O ye religious! discountenance every one among you who shall pretend to despise art and science. I call upon you in the name of Jesus! What is the life of man but art and science? Is it meat and drink? Is not the body more than raiment? What is mortality but the things relating to the body which dies? What is immortality but the things relating to the spirit which lives immortally? What is the joy of Heaven but improvement in the things of the spirit? What are the pains of Hell but ignorance, idleness, bodily lust, and the devastation of the things of the spirit? Answer this for yourselves, and expel from amongst you those who pretend to despise the labours of art and science, which alone are the labours of the gospel. Is not this plain and manifest to the thought? Can you think at all, and not pronounce heartily that to labour in knowledge is to build Jerusalem, and to despise knowledge is to despise Jerusalem and her builders? And remember, he who despises and mocks a mental gift in another, calling it pride, and selfishness, and sin, mocks Jesus, the giver of every mental gift, which always appear to the ignorance-loving hypocrites as sins. But that which is sin in the sight of cruel man is not sin in the sight of our kind God. Let every Christian as much as in him lies engage himself openly and publicly before all the world in some mental pursuit for the building of Jerusalem.' I have given the whole of this long passage because, though the very keystone of his thought, it is little known, being sunk, like nearly all of his most profound thoughts, in the mysterious prophetic books. Obscure about much else, they are always lucid on this one point, and return to it again and again. 'I care not whether a man is good or bad,' are the words they put into the mouth of God, 'all I care is whether he is a wise man or a fool. Go put off holiness and put on intellect.' This cultivated life, which seems to us so artificial a thing, is really, according to them, the laborious re-discovery of the golden age, of the primeval simplicity, of the simple world in which Christ taught and lived, and its lawlessness is the lawlessness of Him 'who being all virtue, acted from impulse and not from rules,'

And his seventy disciples sent
Against religion and government.

The historical Christ was indeed no more than the supreme symbol of the artistic imagination, in which, with every passion wrought to perfect beauty by art and poetry, we shall live, when the body has passed away for the last time; but before that hour man must labour through many lives and many deaths. 'Men are admitted into heaven not because they have curbed and governed their passions, but because they have cultivated their understandings. The treasures of heaven are not negations of passion but realities of intellect from which the passions emanate uncurbed in their eternal glory. The fool shall not enter into heaven, let him be ever so holy. Holiness is not the price of entering into heaven. Those who are cast out are all those who, having no passions of their own, because no intellect, have spent their lives in curbing and governing other people's lives by the various arts of poverty and cruelty of all kinds. The modern Church crucifies Christ with the head downwards. Woe, woe, woe to you hypocrites.' After a time man has 'to return to the dark valley whence he came and begin his labours anew,' but before that return he dwells in the freedom of imagination, in the peace of the 'divine image,' 'the divine vision,' in the peace that passes understanding and is the peace of art. 'I have been very near the gates of death,' Blake wrote in his last letter, 'and have returned very weak and an old man, feeble and tottering but not in spirit and life, not in the real man, the imagination which liveth for ever. In that I grow stronger and stronger as this foolish body decays. . . Flaxman is gone, and we must all soon follow, every one to his eternal home, leaving the delusions of goddess Nature and her laws, to get into freedom from all the laws of the numbers,' the multiplicity of nature, 'into the mind in which every one is king and priest in his own house.' The phrase about the king and priest is a memory of the crown and mitre set upon Dante's head before he entered Paradise. Our imaginations are but fragments of the universal imagination, portions of the universal body of God, and as we enlarge our imagination by imaginative sympathy, and transform with the beauty and peace of art, the sorrows and joys of the world, we put off the limited mortal man more and more and put on the unlimited 'immortal man.' 'As the seed waits eagerly watching for its flower and fruit, anxious its little soul looks out into the clear expanse to see if hungry winds are abroad with their invisible array, so man looks out in tree, and herb, and fish, and bird, and beast, collecting up the fragments of his immortal body into the elemental forms of everything that grows. . . In pain he sighs, in pain he labours in his universe, sorrowing in birds over the deep, or howling in the wolf over the slain, and moaning in the cattle, and in the winds.' Mere sympathy for living things is not enough because we must learn to separate their 'infected' from their eternal, their satanic from their divine part; and this can only be done by desiring always beauty, the one mask through which can be seen the unveiled eyes of eternity. We must then be artists in all things, and understand that love and old age and death are first among the arts. In this sense he insists that 'Christ's apostles were artists,' that 'Christianity is Art,' and that 'the whole business of man is the arts.' Dante, who deified law, selected its antagonist, passion, as the most important of sins, and made the regions where it was punished the largest. Blake, who deified imaginative freedom, held 'corporeal reason' for the most accursed of things, because it makes the imagination revolt from the sovereignty of beauty and pass under the sovereignty of corporeal law, and this is 'the captivity in Egypt.' True art is expressive and symbolic, and makes every form, every sound, every colour, every gesture, a signature of some unanalyzable imaginative essence. False art is not expressive but mimetic, not from experience but from observation, and is the mother of all evil, persuading us to save our bodies alive at no matter what cost of rapine and fraud. True art is the flame of the last day, which begins for every man, when he is first moved by beauty, and which seeks to burn all things until they 'become infinite and holy.'

III. The Illustrations of Dante

THE LATE MR. JOHN ADDINGTON SYMONDS wrote—in a preface to certain Dante illustrations by Stradanus, a sixteenth-century artist

of no great excellence, published in phototype by Mr. Unwin in 1892—
that the illustrations of Gustave Doré, 'in spite of glaring artistic
defects, must, I think, be reckoned first among numerous attempts to
translate Dante's conceptions into terms of plastic art.' One can only
account for this praise of a noisy and demagogic art by supposing that
a temperament, strong enough to explore with unfailing alertness
the countless schools and influences of the Renaissance in Italy, is
of necessity a little lacking in delicacy of judgment and in the finer
substances of emotion. It is more difficult to account for so admirable
a scholar not only preferring these illustrations to the work of what he
called 'the graceful and affected Botticelli,'—although 'Doré was fitted
for his task, not by dramatic vigour, by feeling for beauty, or by anything
sternly in sympathy with the supreme poet's soul, but by a very effective
sense of luminosity and gloom,'—but preferring them because 'he
created a fanciful world, which makes the movement of Dante's *dramatis
personæ* conceivable, introducing the ordinary intelligence into those vast
regions thronged with destinies of souls and creeds and empires.' When
the ordinary student finds this intelligence in an illustrator, he thinks,
because it is his own intelligence, that it is an accurate interpretation
of the text, while work of the extraordinary intelligences is merely an
expression of their own ideas and feelings. Doré and Stradanus, he will
tell you, have given us something of the world of Dante, but Blake and
Botticelli have builded worlds of their own and called them Dante's—as
if Dante's world were more than a mass of symbols of colour and form
and sound which put on humanity, when they arouse some mind to an
intense and romantic life that is not theirs; as if it was not one's own
sorrows and angers and regrets and terrors and hopes that awaken to
condemnation or repentance while Dante treads his eternal pilgrimage;
as if any poet or painter or musician could be other than an enchanter
calling with a persuasive or compelling ritual, creatures, noble or ignoble,
divine or dæmonic, covered with scales or in shining raiment, that he
never imagined, out of the bottomless deeps of imaginations he never
foresaw; as if the noblest achievement of art was not when the artist
enfolds himself in darkness, while he casts over his readers a light as of
a wild and terrible dawn.

Let us therefore put away the designs to *The Divine Comedy*, in which
there is 'an ordinary intelligence,' and consider only the designs in which
the magical ritual has called up extraordinary shapes, the magical light
glimmered upon a world, different from the Dantesque world of our

own intelligence in its ordinary and daily moods, upon a difficult and distinguished world. Most of the series of designs to Dante, and there are a good number, need not busy any one for a moment. Genelli has done a copious series, which is very able in the 'formal' 'generalized' way which Blake hated, and which is spiritually ridiculous. Penelli has transformed the 'Inferno' into a vulgar Walpurgis night, and a certain Schuler, whom I do not find in the biographical dictionaries, but who was apparently a German, has prefaced certain flaccid designs with some excellent charts, while Stradanus has made a series for the 'Inferno,' which has so many of the more material and unessential powers of art, and is so extremely undistinguished in conception, that one supposes him to have touched in the sixteenth century the same public Doré has touched in the nineteenth.

Though with many doubts, I am tempted to value Flaxman's designs to the 'Inferno,' the 'Purgatorio,' and the 'Paradiso,' only a little above the best of these, because he does not seem to have ever been really moved by Dante, and so to have sunk into a formal manner, which is a reflection of the vital manner of his Homer and Hesiod. His designs to *The Divine Comedy* will be laid, one imagines, with some ceremony in that immortal wastepaper-basket in which Time carries with many sighs the failures of great men. I am perhaps wrong, however, because Flaxman even at his best has not yet touched me very deeply, and I hardly ever hope to escape this limitation of my ruling stars. That Signorelli does not seem greatly more interesting except here and there, as in the drawing of 'The Angel,' full of innocence and energy, coming from the boat which has carried so many souls to the foot of the mountain of purgation, can only be because one knows him through poor reproductions from frescoes half mouldered away with damp. A little-known series, drawn by Adolph Stürler, an artist of German extraction, who was settled in Florence in the first half of this century, are very poor in drawing, very pathetic and powerful in invention, and full of most interesting pre-Raphaelitic detail. There are admirable and moving figures, who, having set love above reason, listen in the last abandonment of despair to the judgment of Minos, or walk with a poignant melancholy to the foot of his throne through a land where owls and strange beasts move hither and thither with the sterile content of the evil that neither loves nor hates, and a Cerberus full of patient cruelty. All Stürler's designs have, however, the languor of a mind that does its work by a succession of delicate critical perceptions rather than the decision and energy of true creation, and are more a curious contribution to artistic methods than an imaginative force.

The only designs that compete with Blake's are those of Botticelli and Giulio Clovio, and these contrast rather than compete; for Blake did not live to carry his 'Paradiso' beyond the first faint pencillings, the first thin washes of colour, while Botticelli only, as I think, became supremely imaginative in his 'Paradiso,' and Clovio never attempted the 'Inferno' and 'Purgatorio' at all. The imaginations of Botticelli and Clovio were overshadowed by the cloister, and it was only when they passed beyond the world or into some noble peace, which is not the world's peace, that they won a perfect freedom. Blake had not such mastery over figure and drapery as had Botticelli, but he could sympathize with the persons and delight in the scenery of the 'Inferno' and the 'Purgatorio' as Botticelli could not, and could fill them with a mysterious and spiritual significance born perhaps of mystical pantheism. The flames of Botticelli give one no emotion, and his car of Beatrice is no symbolic chariot of the Church led by the gryphon, half eagle, half lion, of Christ's dual nature, but is a fragment of some mediæval pageant pictured with a merely technical inspiration. Clovio, the illuminator of missals, has tried to create with that too easy hand of his a Paradise of serene air reflected in a little mirror, a heaven of sociability and humility and prettiness, a heaven of women and of monks; but one cannot imagine him deeply moved, as the modern world is moved, by the symbolism of bird and beast, of tree and mountain, of flame and darkness. It was a profound understanding of all creatures and things, a profound sympathy with passionate and lost souls, made possible in their extreme intensity by his revolt against corporeal law, and corporeal reason, which made Blake the one perfectly fit illustrator for the 'Inferno' and the 'Purgatorio': in the serene and rapturous emptiness of Dante's Paradise he would find no symbols but a few abstract emblems, and he had no love for the abstract, while with the drapery and the gestures of Beatrice and Virgil, he would have prospered less than Botticelli or even Clovio.

1897

Symbolism in Painting

In England, which has made great Symbolic Art, most people dislike an art if they are told it is symbolic, for they confuse symbol and allegory. Even Johnson's Dictionary sees no great difference, for it calls a Symbol 'That which comprehends in its figure a representation of something else'; and an Allegory, 'A figurative discourse, in which something other is intended than is contained in the words literally taken.' It is only a very modern Dictionary that calls a Symbol 'the sign or representation of any moral thing by the images or properties of natural things,' which, though an imperfect definition, is not unlike 'The things below are as the things above' of the Emerald Tablet of Hermes! *The Faery Queen* and *The Pilgrim's Progress* have been so important in England that Allegory has overtopped Symbolism, and for a time has overwhelmed it in its own downfall. William Blake was perhaps the first modern to insist on a difference; and the other day, when I sat for my portrait to a German Symbolist in Paris, whose talk was all of his love for Symbolism and his hatred for Allegory, his definitions were the same as William Blake's, of whom he knew nothing. William Blake has written, 'Vision or imagination'—meaning symbolism by these words—'is a representation of what actually exists, really or unchangeably. Fable or Allegory is formed by the daughters of Memory.' The German insisted with many determined gestures, that Symbolism said things which could not be said so perfectly in any other way, and needed but a right instinct for its understanding; while Allegory said things which could be said as well, or better, in another way, and needed a right knowledge for its understanding. The one gave dumb things voices, and bodiless things bodies; while the other read a meaning—which had never lacked its voice or its body—into something heard or seen, and loved less for the meaning than for its own sake. The only symbols he cared for were the shapes and motions of the body; ears hidden by the hair, to make one think of a mind busy with inner voices; and a head so bent that back and neck made the one curve, as in Blake's 'Vision of Bloodthirstiness,' to call up an emotion of bodily strength; and he would not put even a lily, or a rose, or a poppy into a picture to express purity, or love, or sleep, because he thought such emblems were allegorical, and had their meaning by a traditional and not by a natural right. I said that the rose, and the lily, and the poppy were so married, by their colour and their odour, and their use, to love and purity and sleep, or to other symbols of love and purity and sleep, and had been so long a part of the imagination of the world, that a symbolist might use them to help out his meaning without becoming an allegorist. I think I quoted the lily in the hand of the angel in Rossetti's 'Annunciation,' and the lily in the jar in his 'Childhood of Mary Virgin,' and thought they made the more important symbols, the women's bodies, and the angels' bodies, and the clear morning light, take that place, in the great procession of Christian symbols, where they can alone have all their meaning and all their beauty.

It is hard to say where Allegory and Symbolism melt into one another, but it is not hard to say where either comes to its perfection; and though one may doubt whether Allegory or Symbolism is the greater in the horns of Michael Angelo's 'Moses,' one need not doubt that its symbolism has helped to awaken the modern imagination; while Tintoretto's 'Origin of the Milky Way,' which is Allegory without any Symbolism, is, apart from its fine painting, but a moment's amusement for our fancy. A hundred generations might write out what seemed the meaning of the one, and they would write different meanings, for no symbol tells all its meaning to any generation; but when you have said, 'That woman there is Juno, and the milk out of her breast is making the Milky Way,' you have told the meaning of the other, and the fine painting, which has added so much irrelevant beauty, has not told it better.

All Art that is not mere storytelling, or mere portraiture, is symbolic, and has the purpose of those symbolic talismans which mediæval magicians made with complex colours and forms, and bade their patients ponder over daily, and guard with holy secrecy; for it entangles, in complex colours and forms, a part of the Divine Essence. A person or a landscape that is a part of a story or a portrait, evokes but so much emotion as the story or the portrait can permit without loosening the bonds that make it a story or a portrait; but if you liberate a person or a landscape from the bonds of motives and their actions, causes and their effects, and from all bonds but the bonds of your love, it will change under your eyes, and become a symbol of an infinite emotion, a perfected emotion, a part of the Divine Essence; for we love nothing but the perfect, and our dreams make all things perfect, that we may love them. Religious and visionary people, monks and nuns, and medicine-men, and opium-eaters, see symbols in their trances; for religious and visionary thought is thought about perfection and the way to perfection; and symbols are the only things free enough from all bonds to speak of perfection.

Wagner's dramas, Keats' odes, Blake's pictures and poems, Calvert's pictures, Rossetti's pictures, Villiers De l'Isle Adam's plays, and the black-and-white art of Mr. Beardsley and Mr. Ricketts, and the lithographs of Mr. Shannon, and the pictures of Mr. Whistler, and the plays of M. Maeterlinck, and the poetry of Verlaine, in our own day, but differ from the religious art of Giotto and his disciples in having accepted all symbolisms, the symbolism of the ancient shepherds and star-gazers, that symbolism of bodily beauty which seemed a wicked thing to Fra Angelico, the symbolism in day and night, and winter and summer, spring and autumn, once so great a part of an older religion than Christianity; and in having accepted all the Divine Intellect, its anger and its pity, its waking and its sleep, its love and its lust, for the substance of their art. A Keats or a Calvert is as much a symbolist as a Blake or a Wagner; but he is a fragmentary symbolist, for while he evokes in his persons and his landscapes an infinite emotion, a perfected emotion, a part of the Divine Essence, he does not set his symbols in the great procession as Blake would have him, 'in a certain order, suited' to his 'imaginative energy.' If you paint a beautiful woman and fill her face, as Rossetti filled so many faces, with an infinite love, a perfected love, 'one's eyes meet no mortal thing when they meet the light of her peaceful eyes,' as Michael Angelo said of Vittoria Colonna; but one's thoughts stray to mortal things, and ask, maybe, 'Has her lover gone from her, or is he coming?' or 'What pre-destinated unhappiness has made the shadow in her eyes?' If you paint the same face, and set a winged rose or a rose of gold somewhere about her, one's thoughts are of her immortal sisters, Pity and Jealousy, and of her mother, Ancestral Beauty, and of her high kinsmen, the Holy Orders, whose swords make a continual music before her face. The systematic mystic is not the greatest of artists, because his imagination is too great to be bounded by a picture or a song, and because only imperfection in a mirror of perfection, or perfection in a mirror of imperfection, delight our frailty. There is indeed a systematic mystic in every poet or painter who, like Rossetti, delights in a traditional Symbolism, or, like Wagner, delights in a personal Symbolism; and such men often fall into trances, or have waking dreams. Their thought wanders from the woman who is Love herself, to her sisters and her forebears, and to all the great procession; and so august a beauty moves before the mind, that they forget the things which move before the eyes. William Blake, who was the chanticleer of the new dawn, has written: 'If the spectator could enter into one of these images of his imagination, approaching them on the fiery chariot of his contemplative thought, if. . . he could make a friend and companion of one of these images of wonder, which always entreat him to leave mortal things (as he must know), then would he arise from the grave, then would he meet the Lord in the air, and then he would be happy.' And again, 'The world of imagination is the world of Eternity. It is the Divine bosom into which we shall all go after the death of the vegetated body. The world of imagination is infinite and eternal, whereas the world of generation or vegetation is finite and temporal. There exist in that eternal world the eternal realities of everything which we see reflected in the vegetable glass of nature.'

Every visionary knows that the mind's eye soon comes to see a capricious and variable world, which the will cannot shape or change, though it can call it up and banish it again. I closed my eyes a moment ago, and a company of people in blue robes swept by me in a blinding light, and had gone before I had done more than see little roses embroidered on the hems of their robes, and confused, blossoming apple-boughs somewhere beyond them, and recognized one of the company by his square, black curling beard. I have often seen him; and one night a year ago, I asked him questions which he answered by showing me flowers and precious stones, of whose meaning I had no knowledge, and he seemed too perfected a soul for any knowledge that cannot be spoken in symbol or metaphor.

Are he and his blue-robed companions, and their like, 'the Eternal realities' of which we are the reflection 'in the vegetable glass of nature,' or a momentary dream? To answer is to take sides in the only controversy in which it is greatly worth taking sides, and in the only controversy which may never be decided.

1898

The Symbolism of Poetry

I

'Symbolism, as seen in the writers of our day, would have no value if it were not seen also, under one disguise or another, in every great imaginative writer,' writes Mr. Arthur Symons in *The Symbolist Movement in Literature*, a subtle book which I cannot praise as I would, because it has been dedicated to me; and he goes on to show how many profound writers have in the last few years sought for a philosophy of poetry in the doctrine of symbolism, and how even in countries where it is almost scandalous to seek for any philosophy of poetry, new writers are following them in their search. We do not know what the writers of ancient times talked of among themselves, and one bull is all that remains of Shakespeare's talk, who was on the edge of modern times; and the journalist is convinced, it seems, that they talked of wine and women and politics, but never about their art, or never quite seriously about their art. He is certain that no one, who had a philosophy of his art or a theory of how he should write, has ever made a work of art, that people have no imagination who do not write without forethought and afterthought as he writes his own articles. He says this with enthusiasm, because he has heard it at so many comfortable dinner-tables, where some one had mentioned through carelessness, or foolish zeal, a book whose difficulty had offended indolence, or a man who had not forgotten that beauty is an accusation. Those formulas and generalizations, in which a hidden sergeant has drilled the ideas of journalists and through them the ideas of all but all the modern world, have created in their turn a forgetfulness like that of soldiers in battle, so that journalists and their readers have forgotten, among many like events, that Wagner spent seven years arranging and explaining his ideas before he began his most characteristic music; that opera, and with it modern music, arose from certain talks at the house of one Giovanni Bardi of Florence; and that the Pleiade laid the foundations of modern French literature with a pamphlet. Goethe has said, 'a poet needs all philosophy, but he must keep it out of his work,' though that is not always necessary; and certainly he cannot know too much, whether about his own work, or about the procreant waters of the soul where the breath first moved, or about the waters under the earth that are the life of passing things;

and almost certainly no great art, outside England, where journalists are more powerful and ideas less plentiful than elsewhere, has arisen without a great criticism, for its herald or its interpreter and protector, and it is perhaps for this reason that great art, now that vulgarity has armed itself and multiplied itself, is perhaps dead in England.

All writers, all artists of any kind, in so far as they have had any philosophical or critical power, perhaps just in so far as they have been deliberate artists at all, have had some philosophy, some criticism of their art; and it has often been this philosophy, or this criticism, that has evoked their most startling inspiration, calling into outer life some portion of the divine life, of the buried reality, which could alone extinguish in the emotions what their philosophy or their criticism would extinguish in the intellect. They have sought for no new thing, it may be, but only to understand and to copy the pure inspiration of early times, but because the divine life wars upon our outer life, and must needs change its weapons and its movements as we change ours, inspiration has come to them in beautiful startling shapes. The scientific movement brought with it a literature, which was always tending to lose itself in externalities of all kinds, in opinion, in declamation, in picturesque writing, in word-painting, or in what Mr. Symons has called an attempt 'to build in brick and mortar inside the covers of a book'; and now writers have begun to dwell upon the element of evocation, of suggestion, upon what we call the symbolism in great writers.

II

IN 'SYMBOLISM IN PAINTING' I tried to describe the element of symbolism that is in pictures and sculpture, and described a little the symbolism in poetry, but did not describe at all the continuous indefinable symbolism which is the substance of all style.

There are no lines with more melancholy beauty than these by Burns—

> *'The white moon is setting behind the white wave,*
> *And Time is setting with me, O!'*

and these lines are perfectly symbolical. Take from them the whiteness of the moon and of the wave, whose relation to the setting of Time is too subtle for the intellect, and you take from them their beauty. But, when all are together, moon and wave and whiteness and setting Time and the melancholy cry, they evoke an emotion which cannot be evoked by any other arrangement of colours and sounds and forms. We may call this metaphorical writing, but it is better to call it symbolical writing, because metaphors are not profound enough to be moving, when they are not symbols, and when they are symbols they are the most perfect, because the most subtle, outside of pure sound, and through them one can the best find out what symbols are. If one begins the reverie with any beautiful lines that one can remember, one finds they are all like those by Burns. Begin with this line by Blake—

'The gay fishes on the wave when the moon sucks up the dew;'

or these lines by Nash—

> *'Brightness falls from the air,*
> *Queens have died young and fair,*
> *Dust hath closed Helen's eye;'*

or these lines by Shakespeare—

> *'Timon hath made his everlasting mansion*
> *Upon the beached verge of the salt flood;*
> *Who once a day with his embossed froth*
> *The turbulent surge shall cover;'*

or take some line that is quite simple, that gets its beauty from its place in a story, and see how it flickers with the light of the many symbols that have given the story its beauty, as a sword-blade may flicker with the light of burning towers.

All sounds, all colours, all forms, either because of their pre-ordained energies or because of long association, evoke indefinable and yet precise emotions, or, as I prefer to think, call down among us certain disembodied powers, whose footsteps over our hearts we call emotions; and when sound, and colour, and form are in a musical relation, a beautiful relation to one another, they become as it were one sound, one colour, one form, and evoke an emotion that is made out of their distinct evocations and yet is one emotion. The same relation exists between all portions of every work of art, whether it be an epic or a song, and the more perfect it is, and the more various and numerous the elements that have flowed into its perfection, the more powerful will be the emotion, the power, the god it calls among us. Because an emotion does not exist, or does not become perceptible and active among us, till it has found its expression, in colour or in sound or in form, or in all of these, and because no two modulations or arrangements of these evoke the same emotion, poets and painters and musicians, and in a less degree because their effects are momentary, day and night and cloud and shadow, are continually making and unmaking mankind. It is indeed only those things which seem useless or very feeble that have any power, and all those things that seem useful or strong, armies, moving wheels, modes of architecture, modes of government, speculations of the reason, would have been a little different if some mind long ago had not given itself to some emotion, as a woman gives herself to her lover, and shaped sounds or colours or forms, or all of these, into a musical relation, that their emotion might live in other minds. A little lyric evokes an emotion, and this emotion gathers others about it and melts into their being in the making of some great epic; and at last, needing an always less delicate body, or symbol, as it grows more powerful, it flows out, with all it has gathered, among the blind instincts of daily life, where it moves a power within powers, as one sees ring within ring in the stem of an old tree. This is maybe what Arthur O'Shaughnessy meant when he made his poets say they had built Nineveh with their sighing; and I am certainly never certain, when I hear of some war, or of some religious excitement, or of some new manufacture, or of anything else that fills the ear of the world, that it has not all happened because of something that a boy piped in Thessaly. I remember once asking a seer to ask one among the gods who, as she believed, were standing about her in their symbolic bodies, what would come of a charming but seeming trivial labour of a friend, and the form answering, 'the devastation of peoples and the overwhelming of cities.' I doubt indeed if the crude circumstance of the world, which seems to create all our emotions, does more than reflect, as in multiplying mirrors, the emotions that have come to solitary men in moments of poetical contemplation; or that love itself would be more than an animal hunger but for the poet and his shadow the priest, for unless we believe that outer things are the reality, we must believe that the gross is the shadow of the subtle, that things are wise before they become foolish, and secret before they cry out in the market-place. Solitary men in moments of contemplation receive, as I think, the creative impulse from the lowest of the Nine Hierarchies, and so make and unmake mankind, and even the world itself, for does not 'the eye altering alter all'?

> *'Our towns are copied fragments from our breast;*
> *And all man's Babylons strive but to impart*
> *The grandeurs of his Babylonian heart.'*

III

THE PURPOSE OF RHYTHM, IT has always seemed to me, is to prolong the moment of contemplation, the moment when we are both asleep and awake, which is the one moment of creation, by hushing us with an alluring monotony, while it holds us waking by variety, to keep us in that state of perhaps real trance, in which the mind liberated from the pressure of the will is unfolded in symbols. If certain sensitive persons listen persistently to the ticking of a watch, or gaze persistently on the monotonous flashing of a light, they fall into the hypnotic trance; and rhythm is but the ticking of a watch made softer, that one must needs listen, and various, that one may not be swept beyond memory or grow weary of listening; while the patterns of the artist are but the monotonous flash woven to take the eyes in a subtler enchantment. I have heard in meditation voices that were forgotten the moment they had spoken; and I have been swept, when in more profound meditation, beyond all memory but of those things that came from beyond the threshold of waking life. I was writing once at a very symbolical and abstract poem, when my pen fell on the ground; and as I stooped to pick it up, I remembered some phantastic adventure that yet did not seem phantastic, and then another like adventure, and when I asked myself when these things had happened, I found that I was remembering my dreams for many nights. I tried to remember what I had done the day before, and then what I had done that morning; but all my waking life had perished from me, and it was only after a struggle that I came to remember it again, and as I did so that more powerful and startling life perished in its turn. Had my pen not fallen on the ground and so made me turn from the images that I was weaving into verse, I would never have known that meditation had become trance, for I would have been like one who does not know that he is passing through a wood because his eyes are on the pathway. So I think that in the making and in the understanding of a work of art, and the more easily if it is full of patterns and symbols and music, we are lured to the threshold of sleep, and it may be far beyond it, without knowing that we have ever set our feet upon the steps of horn or of ivory.

IV

Besides emotional symbols, symbols that evoke emotions alone,—and in this sense all alluring or hateful things are symbols, although their relations with one another are too subtle to delight us fully, away from rhythm and pattern,—there are intellectual symbols, symbols that evoke ideas alone, or ideas mingled with emotions; and outside the very definite traditions of mysticism and the less definite criticism of certain modern poets, these alone are called symbols. Most things belong to one or another kind, according to the way we speak of them and the companions we give them, for symbols, associated with ideas that are more than fragments of the shadows thrown upon the intellect by the emotions they evoke, are the playthings of the allegorist or the pedant, and soon pass away. If I say 'white' or 'purple' in an ordinary line of poetry, they evoke emotions so exclusively that I cannot say why they move me; but if I say them in the same mood, in the same breath with such obvious intellectual symbols as a cross or a crown of thorns, I think of purity and sovereignty; while innumerable other meanings, which are held to one another by the bondage of subtle suggestion, and alike in the emotions and in the intellect, move visibly through my mind, and move invisibly beyond the threshold of sleep, casting lights and shadows of an indefinable wisdom on what had seemed before, it may be, but sterility and noisy violence. It is the intellect that decides where the reader shall ponder over the procession of the symbols, and if the symbols are merely emotional, he gazes from amid the accidents and destinies of the world; but if the symbols are intellectual too, he becomes himself a part of pure intellect, and he is himself mingled with the procession. If I watch a rushy pool in the moonlight, my emotion at its beauty is mixed with memories of the man that I have seen ploughing by its margin, or of the lovers I saw there a night ago; but if I look at the moon herself and remember any of her ancient names and meanings, I move among divine people, and things that have shaken off our mortality, the tower of ivory, the queen of waters, the shining stag among enchanted woods, the white hare sitting upon the hilltop, the fool of faery with his shining cup full of dreams, and it may be 'make a friend of one of these images of wonder,' and 'meet the Lord in the air.' So, too, if one is moved by Shakespeare, who is content with emotional symbols that he may come the nearer to our sympathy, one is mixed with the whole spectacle of the world; while if one is moved by Dante, or by the myth of Demeter, one is mixed into the shadow of God or of a goddess. So too one is furthest from symbols when one is busy doing this or that, but the soul moves among symbols and unfolds in symbols when trance, or madness, or deep meditation has withdrawn it from every impulse but its own. 'I then saw,' wrote Gérard de Nerval of his madness, 'vaguely drifting into form, plastic images of antiquity, which outlined themselves, became definite, and seemed to represent symbols of which I only seized the idea with difficulty.' In an earlier time he would have been of that multitude, whose souls austerity withdrew, even more perfectly than madness could withdraw his soul, from hope and memory, from desire and regret, that they might reveal those processions of symbols that men bow to before altars, and woo with incense and offerings. But being of our time, he has been like Maeterlinck, like Villiers de l'Isle Adam in *Axël*, like all who are preoccupied with intellectual symbols in our time, a foreshadower of the new sacred book, of which all the arts, as somebody has said, are begging to dream, and because, as I think, they cannot overcome the slow dying of men's hearts that we call the progress of the world, and lay their hands upon men's heart-strings again, without becoming the garment of religion as in old times.

V

IF PEOPLE WERE TO ACCEPT the theory that poetry moves us because of its symbolism, what change should one look for in the manner of our poetry? A return to the way of our fathers, a casting out of descriptions of nature for the sake of nature, of the moral law for the sake of the moral law, a casting out of all anecdotes and of that brooding over scientific opinion that so often extinguished the central flame in Tennyson, and of that vehemence that would make us do or not do certain things; or, in other words, we should come to understand that the beryl stone was enchanted by our fathers that it might unfold the pictures in its heart, and not to mirror our own excited faces, or the boughs waving outside the window. With this change of substance, this return to imagination, this understanding that the laws of art, which are the hidden laws of the world, can alone bind the imagination, would come a change of style, and we would cast out of serious poetry those energetic rhythms, as of a man running, which are the invention of the will with its eyes always on something to be done or undone; and we would seek out those wavering, meditative, organic rhythms, which are the embodiment of the imagination, that neither desires nor hates, because it has done with time, and only wishes to gaze upon some reality, some beauty; nor would it be any longer possible for anybody to deny the importance of form, in all its kinds, for although you can expound an opinion, or describe a thing when your words are not quite well chosen, you cannot give a body to something that moves beyond the senses, unless your words are as subtle, as complex, as full of mysterious life, as the body of a flower or of a woman. The form of sincere poetry, unlike the form of the popular poetry, may indeed be sometimes obscure, or ungrammatical as in some of the best of the Songs of Innocence and Experience, but it must have the perfections that escape analysis, the subtleties that have a new meaning every day, and it must have all this whether it be but a little song made out of a moment of dreamy indolence, or some great epic made out of the dreams of one poet and of a hundred generations whose hands were never weary of the sword.

1900

The Theatre

I

I REMEMBER, SOME YEARS AGO, advising a distinguished, though too little recognized, writer of poetical plays to write a play as unlike ordinary plays as possible, that it might be judged with a fresh mind, and to put it on the stage in some small suburban theatre, where a small audience would pay its expenses. I said that he should follow it the year after, at the same time of the year, with another play, and so on from year to year; and that the people who read books, and do not go to the theatre, would gradually find out about him. I suggested that he should begin with a pastoral play, because nobody would expect from a pastoral play the succession of nervous tremours which the plays of commerce, like the novels of commerce, have substituted for the purification that comes with pity and terror to the imagination and intellect. He followed my advice in part, and had a small but perfect success, filling his small theatre for twice the number of performances he had announced; but instead of being content with the praise of his equals, and waiting to win their praise another year, he hired immediately a big London theatre, and put his pastoral play and a new play before a meagre and unintelligent audience. I still remember his pastoral play with delight, because, if not always of a high excellence, it was always poetical; but I remember it at the small theatre, where my pleasure was magnified by the pleasure of those about me, and not at the big theatre, where it made me uncomfortable, as an unwelcome guest always makes one uncomfortable.

Why should we thrust our works, which we have written with imaginative sincerity and filled with spiritual desire, before those quite excellent people who think that Rossetti's women are 'guys,' that Rodin's women are 'ugly,' and that Ibsen is 'immoral,' and who only want to be left at peace to enjoy the works so many clever men have made especially to suit them? We must make a theatre for ourselves and our friends, and for a few simple people who understand from sheer simplicity what we understand from scholarship and thought. We have planned the Irish Literary Theatre with this hospitable emotion, and, that the right people may find out about us, we hope to act a play or two in the spring of every year; and that the right people may escape the stupefying memory of the theatre of commerce which clings even to them, our plays will be for the most part remote, spiritual, and ideal.

A common opinion is that the poetic drama has come to an end, because modern poets have no dramatic power; and Mr. Binyon seems to accept this opinion when he says: 'It has been too often assumed that it is the manager who bars the way to poetic plays. But it is much more probable that the poets have failed the managers. If poets mean to serve the stage, their dramas must be dramatic.' I find it easier to believe that audiences, who have learned, as I think, from the life of crowded cities to live upon the surface of life, and actors and managers, who study to please them, have changed, than that imagination, which is the voice of what is eternal in man, has changed. The arts are but one Art; and why should all intense painting and all intense poetry have become not merely unintelligible but hateful to the greater number of men and women, and intense drama move them to pleasure? The audiences of Sophocles and of Shakespeare and of Calderon were not unlike the audiences I have heard listening in Irish cabins to songs in Gaelic about 'an old poet telling his sins,' and about 'the five young men who were drowned last year,' and about 'the lovers that were drowned going to America,' or to some tale of Oisin and his three hundred years in *Tir nan Oge*. Mr. Bridges' *Return of Ulysses*, one of the most beautiful and, as I think, dramatic of modern plays, might have some success in the Aran Islands, if the Gaelic League would translate it into Gaelic, but I am quite certain that it would have no success in the Strand.

Blake has said that all Art is a labour to bring again the Golden Age, and all culture is certainly a labour to bring again the simplicity of the first ages, with knowledge of good and evil added to it. The drama has need of cities that it may find men in sufficient numbers, and cities destroy the emotions to which it appeals, and therefore the days of the drama are brief and come but seldom. It has one day when the emotions of cities still remember the emotions of sailors and husbandmen and shepherds and users of the spear and the bow; as the houses and furniture and earthen vessels of cities, before the coming of machinery, remember the rocks and the woods and the hillside; and it has another day, now beginning, when thought and scholarship discover their desire. In the first day, it is the Art of the people; and in the second day, like the dramas acted of old times in the hidden places of temples, it is the preparation of a Priesthood. It may be, though the world is not old enough to show us any example, that this Priesthood will spread their Religion everywhere, and make their Art the Art of the people.

When the first day of the drama had passed by, actors found that an always larger number of people were more easily moved through the eyes than through the ears. The emotion that comes with the music of words is exhausting, like all intellectual emotions, and few people like exhausting emotions; and therefore actors began to speak as if they were reading something out of the newspapers. They forgot the noble art of oratory, and gave all their thought to the poor art of acting, that is content with the sympathy of our nerves; until at last those who love poetry found it better to read alone in their rooms what they had once delighted to hear sitting friend by friend, lover by beloved. I once asked Mr. William Morris if he had thought of writing a play, and he answered that he had, but would not write one, because actors did not know how to speak poetry with the half-chant men spoke it with in old times. Mr. Swinburne's *Locrine* was acted a month ago, and it was not badly acted, but nobody could tell whether it was fit for the stage or not, for not one rhythm, not one cry of passion, was spoken with a musical emphasis, and verse spoken without a musical emphasis seems but an artificial and cumbersome way of saying what might be said naturally and simply in prose.

As audiences and actors changed, managers learned to substitute meretricious landscapes, painted upon wood and canvas, for the descriptions of poetry, until the painted scenery, which had in Greece been a charming explanation of what was least important in the story, became as important as the story. It needed some imagination, some gift for day-dreams, to see the horses and the fields and flowers of Colonus as one listened to the elders gathered about OEdipus, or to see 'the pendent bed and procreant cradle' of the 'martlet' as one listened to Duncan before the castle of Macbeth; but it needs no imagination to admire a painting of one of the more obvious effects of nature painted by somebody who understands how to show everything to the most hurried glance. At the same time the managers made the costumes of the actors more and more magnificent, that the mind might sleep in peace, while the eye took pleasure in the magnificence of velvet and silk and in the physical beauty of women. These changes gradually perfected the theatre of commerce, the masterpiece of that movement towards externality in life and thought and Art, against which the criticism of our day is learning to protest.

Even if poetry were spoken as poetry, it would still seem out of place in many of its highest moments upon a stage, where the superficial appearances of nature are so closely copied; for poetry is founded upon convention, and becomes incredible the moment painting or gesture remind us that people do not speak verse when they meet upon the highway. The theatre of Art, when it comes to exist, must therefore discover grave and decorative gestures, such as delighted Rossetti and Madox Brown, and grave and decorative scenery, that will be forgotten the moment an actor has said 'It is dawn,' or 'It is raining,' or 'The wind is shaking the trees'; and dresses of so little irrelevant magnificence that the mortal actors and actresses may change without much labour into the immortal people of romance. The theatre began in ritual, and it cannot come to its greatness again without recalling words to their ancient sovereignty.

It will take a generation, and perhaps generations, to restore the theatre of Art; for one must get one's actors, and perhaps one's scenery, from the theatre of commerce, until new actors and new painters have come to help one; and until many failures and imperfect successes have made a new tradition, and perfected in detail the ideal that is beginning to float before our eyes. If one could call one's painters and one's actors from where one would, how easy it would be. I know some painters, who have never painted scenery, who could paint the scenery I want, but they have their own work to do; and in Ireland I have heard a red-haired orator repeat some bad political verses with a voice that went through one like flame, and made them seem the most beautiful verses in the world; but he has no practical knowledge of the stage, and probably despises it.

May 1899

II

DIONYSIUS, THE AREOPAGITE, WROTE THAT 'He has set the borders of the nations according to His angels.' It is these angels, each one the genius of some race about to be unfolded, that are the founders of intellectual traditions; and as lovers understand in their first glance all that is to befall them, and as poets and musicians see the whole work in its first impulse, so races prophesy at their awakening whatever the generations that are to prolong their traditions shall accomplish in detail. It is only at the awakening—as in ancient Greece, or in Elizabethan England, or in contemporary Scandinavia—that great numbers of men understand that a right understanding of life and of destiny is more important than amusement. In London, where all the intellectual traditions gather to die, men hate a play if they are told it is literature, for they will not endure a spiritual superiority; but in Athens, where so many intellectual traditions were born, Euripides once changed hostility to enthusiasm by asking his playgoers whether it was his business to teach them, or their business to teach him. New races understand instinctively, because the future cries in their ears, that the old revelations are insufficient, and that all life is revelation beginning in miracle and enthusiasm, and dying out as it unfolds itself in what we have mistaken for progress. It is one of our illusions, as I think, that education, the softening of manners, the perfecting of law—countless images of a fading light—can create nobleness and beauty, and that life moves slowly and evenly towards some perfection. Progress is miracle, and it is sudden, because miracles are the work of an all-powerful energy, and nature in herself has no power except to die and to forget. If one studies one's own mind, one comes to think with Blake, that 'every time less than a pulsation of the artery is equal to six thousand years, for in this period the poet's work is done; and all the great events of time start forth and are conceived in such a period, within a pulsation of the artery.'

February 1900

The Celtic Element in Literature

I

Ernest Renan described what he held to be Celtic characteristics in *The Poetry of the Celtic Races*. I must repeat the well-known sentences: 'No race communed so intimately as the Celtic race with the lower creation, or believed it to have so big a share of moral life.' The Celtic race had 'a realistic naturalism,' 'a love of nature for herself, a vivid feeling for her magic, commingled with the melancholy a man knows when he is face to face with her, and thinks he hears her communing with him about his origin and his destiny.' 'It has worn itself out in mistaking dreams for realities,' and 'compared with the classical imagination the Celtic imagination is indeed the infinite contrasted with the finite.' 'Its history is one long lament, it still recalls its exiles, its flights across the seas.' 'If at times it seems to be cheerful, its tear is not slow to glisten behind the smile. Its songs of joy end as elegies; there is nothing to equal the delightful sadness of its national melodies.' Matthew Arnold, in *The Study of Celtic Literature*, has accepted this passion for nature, this imaginativeness, this melancholy, as Celtic characteristics, but has described them more elaborately. The Celtic passion for nature comes almost more from a sense of her 'mystery' than of her 'beauty,' and it adds 'charm and magic' to nature, and the Celtic imaginativeness and melancholy are alike 'a passionate, turbulent, indomitable reaction against the despotism of fact.' The Celt is not melancholy, as Faust or Werther are melancholy, from 'a perfectly definite motive,' but because of something about him 'unaccountable, defiant and titanic.' How well one knows these sentences, better even than Renan's, and how well one knows the passages of prose and verse which he uses to prove that wherever English literature has the qualities these sentences describe, it has them from a Celtic source. Though I do not think any of us who write about Ireland have built any argument upon them, it is well to consider them a little, and see where they are helpful and where they are hurtful. If we do not, we may go mad some day, and the enemy root up our rose-garden and plant a cabbage-garden instead. Perhaps we must restate a little, Renan's and Arnold's argument.

II

ONCE EVERY PEOPLE IN THE world believed that trees were divine, and could take a human or grotesque shape and dance among the shadows; and that deer, and ravens and foxes, and wolves and bears, and clouds and pools, almost all things under the sun and moon, and the sun and moon, were not less divine and changeable. They saw in the rainbow the still bent bow of a god thrown down in his negligence; they heard in the thunder the sound of his beaten water-jar, or the tumult of his chariot wheels; and when a sudden flight of wild duck, or of crows, passed over their heads, they thought they were gazing at the dead hastening to their rest; while they dreamed of so great a mystery in little things that they believed the waving of a hand, or of a sacred bough, enough to trouble far-off hearts, or hood the moon with darkness. All old literatures are full of these or of like imaginations, and all the poets of races, who have not lost this way of looking at things, could have said of themselves, as the poet of the *Kalevala* said of himself, 'I have learned my songs from the music of many birds, and from the music of many waters.' When a mother in the *Kalevala* weeps for a daughter, who was drowned flying from an old suitor, she weeps so greatly that her tears become three rivers, and cast up three rocks, on which grow three birch-trees, where three cuckoos sit and sing, the one 'love, love,' the one 'suitor, suitor,' the one 'consolation, consolation.' And the makers of the Sagas made the squirrel run up and down the sacred ash-tree carrying words of hatred from the eagle to the worm, and from the worm to the eagle; although they had less of the old way than the makers of the *Kalavala*, for they lived in a more crowded and complicated world, and were learning the abstract meditation which lures men from visible beauty, and were unlearning, it may be, the impassioned meditation which brings men beyond the edge of trance and makes trees, and beasts, and dead things talk with human voices.

The old Irish and the old Welsh, though they had less of the old way than the makers of the *Kalavala*, had more of it than the makers of the Sagas, and it is this that distinguishes the examples Matthew Arnold quotes of their 'natural magic,' of their sense of 'the mystery' more than of 'the beauty' of nature. When Matthew Arnold wrote it was not easy to know as much as we know now of folk song and folk belief, and I do not think he understood that our 'natural magic' is but the ancient religion of the world, the ancient worship of nature and that troubled ecstasy before her, that certainty of all beautiful places being haunted, which it brought into men's minds. The ancient religion is in that passage of the *Mabinogion* about the making of 'Flower Aspect.' Gwydion and Math made her 'by charms and illusions' 'out of flowers.' 'They took the blossoms of the oak, and the blossoms of the broom, and the blossoms of the meadow-sweet, and produced from them a maiden the fairest and most graceful that man ever saw; and they baptized her, and called her Flower Aspect'; and one finds it in the not less beautiful passage about the burning Tree, that has half its beauty from calling up a fancy of leaves so living and beautiful, they can be of no less living and beautiful a thing than flame: 'They saw a tall tree by the side of the river, one half of which was in flames from the root to the top, and the other half was green and in full leaf.' And one finds it very certainly in the quotations he makes from English poets to prove a Celtic influence in English poetry; in Keats's 'magic casements opening on the foam of perilous seas in faery lands forlorn'; in his 'moving waters at their priest-like task of pure ablution round earth's human shore'; in Shakespeare's 'floor of heaven,' 'inlaid with patens of bright gold'; and in his Dido standing 'on the wild sea banks,' 'a willow in her hand,' and waving it in the ritual of the old worship of nature and the spirits of nature, to wave 'her love to come again to Carthage.' And his other examples have the delight and wonder of devout worshippers among the haunts of their divinities. Is there not such delight and wonder in the description of Olwen in the *Mabinogion*: 'More yellow was her hair than the flower of the broom, and her skin was whiter than the foam of the wave, and fairer were her hands and her fingers than the blossoms of the wood-anemone amidst the spray of the meadow fountains.' And is there not such delight and wonder in—

> *'Meet we on hill, in dale, forest, or mead,*
> *By paved fountain or by rushy brook,*
> *Or on the beached margent of the sea'?*

If men had never dreamed that fair women could be made out of flowers, or rise up out of meadow fountains and paved fountains, neither passage could have been written. Certainly, the descriptions of nature made in what Matthew Arnold calls 'the faithful way,' or in what he calls 'the Greek way,' would have lost nothing if all the meadow fountains or paved fountains were meadow fountains and paved fountains and nothing more. When Keats wrote, in the Greek way, which adds lightness and brightness to nature—

> *'What little town by river or sea-shore*
> *Or mountain built with quiet citadel,*
> *Is emptied of its folk, this pious morn';*

when Shakespeare wrote in the Greek way—

> *'I know a bank where the wild thyme blows,*
> *Where oxlips and the nodding violet grows';*

when Virgil wrote in the Greek way—

> *'Muscosi fontes et somno mollior herba,'*

and

> *'Pallentes violas et summa papavera carpens*
> *Narcissum et florem jungit bene olentis anethi';*

they looked at nature without ecstasy, but with the affection a man feels for the garden where he has walked daily and thought pleasant thoughts. They looked at nature in the modern way, the way of people who are poetical, but are more interested in one another than in a nature which has faded to be but friendly and pleasant, the way of people who have forgotten the ancient religion.

III

MEN WHO LIVED IN A world where anything might flow and change, and become any other thing; and among great gods whose passions were in the flaming sunset, and in the thunder and the thunder-shower, had not our thoughts of weight and measure. They worshipped nature and the abundance of nature, and had always, as it seems, for a supreme ritual that tumultuous dance among the hills or in the depths of the woods, where unearthly ecstasy fell upon the dancers, until they seemed the gods or the godlike beasts, and felt their souls overtopping the moon; and, as some think, imagined for the first time in the world the blessed country of the gods and of the happy dead. They had imaginative passions because they did not live within our own strait limits, and were nearer to ancient chaos, every man's desire, and had immortal models about them. The hare that ran by among the dew might have sat upon his haunches when the first man was made, and the poor bunch of rushes under their feet might have been a goddess laughing among the stars; and with but a little magic, a little waving of the hands, a little murmuring of the lips, they too could become a hare or a bunch of rushes, and know immortal love and immortal hatred.

All folk literature, and all literature that keeps the folk tradition, delights in unbounded and immortal things. The *Kalevala* delights in the seven hundred years that Luonaton wanders in the depths of the sea with Wäinämöinen in her womb, and the Mahomedan king in the Song of Roland, pondering upon the greatness of Charlemagne, repeats over and over, 'He is three hundred years old, when will he weary of war?' Cuchulain in the Irish folk tale had the passion of victory, and he overcame all men, and died warring upon the waves, because they alone had the strength to overcome him. The lover in the Irish folk song bids his beloved come with him into the woods, and see the salmon leap in the rivers, and hear the cuckoo sing, because death will never find them in the heart of the woods. Oisin, new come from his three hundred years of faeryland, and of the love that is in faeryland, bids St. Patrick cease his prayers a while and listen to the blackbird, because it is the blackbird of Darrycarn that Finn brought from Norway, three hundred years before, and set its nest upon the oak-tree with his own hands. Surely if one goes far enough into the woods, one will find there all that one is seeking? Who knows how many centuries the birds of the woods have been singing?

All folk literature has indeed a passion whose like is not in modern literature and music and art, except where it has come by some straight or crooked way out of ancient times. Love was held to be a fatal sickness in ancient Ireland, and there is a love-poem in *The Songs of Connacht* that is like a death cry: 'My love, O she is my love, the woman who is most for destroying me, dearer is she for making me ill than the woman who would be for making me well. She is my treasure, O she is my treasure, the woman of the grey eyes. . . a woman who would not lay a hand under my head. . . She is my love, O she is my love, the woman who left no strength in me; a woman who would not breathe a sigh after me, a woman who would not raise a stone at my tomb. . .

She is my secret love, O she is my secret love. A woman who tells me nothing, . . . a woman who does not remember me to be out. . . She is my choice, O she is my choice, the woman who would not look back at me, the woman who would not make peace with me. . . She is my desire, O she is my desire: a woman dearest to me under the sun, a woman who would not pay me heed, if I were to sit by her side. It is she ruined my heart and left a sigh for ever in me.' There is another song that ends, 'The Erne shall be in strong flood, the hills shall be torn down, and the sea shall have red waves, and blood shall be spilled, and every mountain valley and every moor shall be on high, before you shall perish, my little black rose.' Nor do the old Irish weigh and measure their hatred. The nurse of O'Sullivan Bere in the folk song prays that the bed of his betrayer may be the red hearth-stone of hell for ever. And an Elizabethan Irish poet cries: 'Three things are waiting for my death. The devil, who is waiting for my soul and cares nothing for my body or my wealth; the worms, who are waiting for my body but care nothing for my soul or my wealth; my children, who are waiting for my wealth and care nothing for my body or my soul. O Christ, hang all three in the one noose.' Such love and hatred seek no mortal thing but their own infinity, and such love and hatred soon become love and hatred of the idea. The lover who loves so passionately can soon sing to his beloved like the lover in the poem by 'A. E.,' 'A vast desire awakes and grows into forgetfulness of thee.'

When an early Irish poet calls the Irishman famous for much loving, and a proverb, a friend has heard in the Highlands of Scotland, talks of the lovelessness of the Irishman, they may say but the same thing, for if your passion is but great enough it leads you to a country where there are many cloisters. The hater who hates with too good a heart soon comes also to hate the idea only; and from this idealism in love and hatred comes, as I think, a certain power of saying and forgetting things, especially a power of saying and forgetting things in politics, which others do not say and forget. The ancient farmers and herdsmen were full of love and hatred, and made their friends gods, and their enemies the enemies of gods, and those who keep their tradition are not less mythological. From this 'mistaking dreams,' which are perhaps essences, for 'realities' which are perhaps accidents, from this 'passionate, turbulent reaction against the despotism of fact,' comes, it may be, that melancholy which made all ancient peoples delight in tales that end in death and parting, as modern peoples delight in tales that end in marriage bells; and made all ancient peoples, who like the old Irish had a nature more lyrical than dramatic, delight in wild and beautiful lamentations. Life was so weighed down by the emptiness of the great forests and by the mystery of all things, and by the greatness of its own desires, and, as I think, by the loneliness of much beauty; and seemed so little and so fragile and so brief, that nothing could be more sweet in the memory than a tale that ended in death and parting, and than a wild and beautiful lamentation. Men did not mourn merely because their beloved was married to another, or because learning was bitter in the mouth, for such mourning believes that life might be happy were it different, and is therefore the less mourning; but because they had been born and must die with their great thirst unslaked. And so it is that all the august sorrowful persons of literature, Cassandra and Helen and Deirdre, and Lear and Tristan, have come out of legends and are indeed but the images of the primitive imagination mirrored in the little looking-glass of the modern and classic imagination. This is that 'melancholy a man knows when he is face to face' with nature, and thinks 'he hears her communing with him about' the mournfulness of being born and of dying; and how can it do otherwise than call into his mind 'its exiles, its flights across the seas,' that it may stir the ever-smouldering ashes? No Gaelic poetry is so popular in Gaelic-speaking places as the lamentations of Oisin, old and miserable, remembering the companions and the loves of his youth, and his three hundred years in faeryland, and his faery love: all dreams withering in the winds of time lament in his lamentations: 'The clouds are long above me this night; last night was a long night to me; although I find this day long, yesterday was still longer. Every day that comes to me is long. . . No one in this great world is like me—a poor old man dragging stones. The clouds are long above me this night. I am the last man of the Fianna, the great Oisin, the son of Finn, listening to the sound of bells. The clouds are long above me this night.' Matthew Arnold quotes the lamentation of Leyrach Hen as a type of the Celtic melancholy, but I prefer to quote it as a type of the primitive melancholy; 'O my crutch, is it not autumn when the fern is red and the water flag yellow? Have I not hated that which I love? . . . Behold, old age, which makes sport of me, from the hair of my head and my teeth, to my eyes which women loved. The four things I have all my life most hated fall upon me together—coughing and old age, sickness and sorrow. I am old, I am alone, shapeliness and warmth are gone from me, the couch of honour shall be no more mine; I am miserable, I am bent on my crutch. How evil was the lot allotted to Leyrach, the night he was brought forth! Sorrows without end and no deliverance from his burden.' An Elizabethan writer describes extravagant sorrow by calling it 'to weep Irish'; and Oisin and Leyrach Hen are, I think, a little nearer even to us modern Irish than they are to most people. That is why our poetry and much of our thought is melancholy. 'The same man,' writes Dr. Hyde in the beautiful prose which he first writes in Gaelic, 'who will to-day be dancing, sporting, drinking, and shouting, will be soliloquizing by himself to-morrow, heavy and sick and sad in his own lonely little hut, making a croon over departed hopes, lost life, the vanity of this world, and the coming of death.'

IV

MATTHEW ARNOLD ASKS HOW MUCH of the Celt must one imagine in the ideal man of genius. I prefer to say, how much of the ancient hunters and fishers and of the ecstatic dancers among hills and woods must one imagine in the ideal man of genius. Certainly a thirst for unbounded emotion and a wild melancholy are troublesome things in the world, and do not make its life more easy or orderly, but it may be the arts are founded on the life beyond the world, and that they must cry in the ears of our penury until the world has been consumed and become a vision. Certainly, as Samuel Palmer wrote, 'Excess is the vivifying spirit of the finest art, and we must always seek to make excess more abundantly excessive.' Matthew Arnold has said that if he were asked 'where English got its turn for melancholy and its turn for natural magic,' he 'would answer with little doubt that it got much of its melancholy from a Celtic source, with no doubt at all that from a Celtic source is got nearly all its natural magic.'

I will put this differently and say that literature dwindles to a mere chronicle of circumstance, or passionless phantasies, and passionless meditations, unless it is constantly flooded with the passions and beliefs of ancient times, and that of all the fountains of the passions and beliefs of ancient times in Europe, the Sclavonic, the Finnish, the Scandinavian, and the Celtic, the Celtic alone has been for centuries close to the main river of European literature. It has again and again brought 'the vivifying spirit' 'of excess' into the arts of Europe. Ernest Renan has told how the visions of purgatory seen by pilgrims to Lough

Derg—once visions of the pagan under-world, as the boat made out of a hollow tree that bore the pilgrim to the holy island were alone enough to prove—gave European thought new symbols of a more abundant penitence; and had so great an influence that he has written, 'It cannot be doubted for a moment that to the number of poetical themes Europe owes to the genius of the Celt is to be added the framework of the divine comedy.'

A little later the legends of Arthur and his table, and of the Holy Grail, once it seems the cauldron of an Irish God, changed the literature of Europe, and it may be changed, as it were, the very roots of man's emotions by their influence on the spirit of chivalry and on the spirit of romance; and later still Shakespeare found his Mab, and probably his Puck, and one knows not how much else of his faery kingdom, in Celtic legend; while at the beginning of our own day Sir Walter Scott gave Highland legends and Highland excitability so great a mastery over all romance that they seem romance herself.

In our own time Scandinavian tradition, because of the imagination of Richard Wagner and of William Morris and of the earlier and, as I think, greater Heinrich Ibsen, has created a new romance, and through the imagination of Richard Wagner, become all but the most passionate element in the arts of the modern world. There is indeed but one other element as passionate, the still unfaded legends of Arthur and of the Holy Grail; and now a new fountain of legends, and, as I think, a more abundant fountain than any in Europe, is being opened, the great fountain of Gaelic legends; the tale of Deirdre, who alone among the women who have set men mad was at once the white flame and the red flame, wisdom and loveliness; the tale of the Sons of Tuireann, with its unintelligible mysteries, an old Grail Quest as I think; the tale of the four children changed into four swans, and lamenting over many waters; the tale of the love of Cuchulain for an immortal goddess, and his coming home to a mortal woman in the end; the tale of his many battles at the ford with that dear friend he kissed before the battles, and over whose dead body he wept when he had killed him; the tale of his death and of the lamentations of Emer; the tale of the flight of Grainne with Diarmuid, strangest of all tales of the fickleness of woman, and the tale of the coming of Oisin out of faeryland, and of his memories and lamentations. 'The Celtic movement,' as I understand it, is principally the opening of this fountain, and none can measure of how great importance it may be to coming times, for every new fountain of legends

WILLIAM BUTLER YEATS

is a new intoxication for the imagination of the world. It comes at a time when the imagination of the world is as ready, as it was at the coming of the tales of Arthur and of the Grail, for a new intoxication. The reaction against the rationalism of the eighteenth century has mingled with a reaction against the materialism of the nineteenth century, and the symbolical movement, which has come to perfection in Germany in Wagner, in England in the Pre-Raphaelites, and in France in Villiers De l'Isle Adam, and Mallarmé, and Maeterlinck, and has stirred the imagination of Ibsen and D'Annunzio, is certainly the only movement that is saying new things. The arts by brooding upon their own intensity have become religious, and are seeking, as I think Verhaeren has said, to create a sacred book. They must, as religious thought has always done, utter themselves through legends; and the Sclavonic and Finnish legends tell of strange woods and seas, and the Scandinavian legends are held by a great master, and tell also of strange woods and seas, and the Welsh legends are held by almost as many great masters as the Greek legends, while the Irish legends move among known woods and seas, and have so much of a new beauty, that they may well give the opening century its most memorable symbols.

1897

I could have written this essay with much more precision and have much better illustrated my meaning if I had waited until Lady Gregory had finished her book of legends, *Cuchulain of Muirthemne*, a book to set beside the *Morte D'Arthur* and the *Mabinogion*.

1902

The Autumn of the Body

Our thoughts and emotions are often but spray flung up from hidden tides that follow a moon no eye can see. I remember that when I first began to write I desired to describe outward things as vividly as possible, and took pleasure, in which there was, perhaps, a little discontent, in picturesque and declamatory books. And then quite suddenly I lost the desire of describing outward things, and found that I took little pleasure in a book unless it was spiritual and unemphatic. I did not then understand that the change was from beyond my own mind, but I understand now that writers are struggling all over Europe, though not often with a philosophic understanding of their struggle, against that picturesque and declamatory way of writing, against that 'externality' which a time of scientific and political thought has brought into literature. This struggle has been going on for some years, but it has only just become strong enough to draw within itself the little inner world which alone seeks more than amusement in the arts. In France, where movements are more marked, because the people are pre-eminently logical, *The Temptation of S. Anthony*, the last great dramatic invention of the old romanticism, contrasts very plainly with *Axël*, the first great dramatic invention of the new; and Maeterlinck has followed Count Villiers de l'Isle Adam. Flaubert wrote unforgettable descriptions of grotesque, bizarre, and beautiful scenes and persons, as they show to the ear and to the eye, and crowded them with historic and ethnographical details; but Count Villiers de l'Isle Adam swept together, by what seemed a sudden energy, words behind which glimmered a spiritual and passionate mood, as the flame glimmers behind the dusky blue and red glass in an Eastern lamp; and created persons from whom has fallen all even of personal characteristic except a thirst for that hour when all things shall pass away like a cloud, and a pride like that of the Magi following their star over many mountains; while Maeterlinck has plucked away even this thirst and this pride and set before us faint souls, naked and pathetic shadows already half vapour and sighing to one another upon the border of the last abyss. There has been, as I think, a like change in French painting, for one sees everywhere, instead of the dramatic stories and picturesque moments of an older school, frail and tremulous bodies unfitted for the labour of life, and landscape where subtle rhythms of colour and of form have overcome the clear outline of things as we see them in the labour of life.

There has been a like change in England, but it has come more gradually and is more mixed with lesser changes than in France. The poetry which found its expression in the poems of writers like Browning and of Tennyson, and even of writers, who are seldom classed with them, like Swinburne, and like Shelley in his earlier years, pushed its limits as far as possible, and tried to absorb into itself the science and politics, the philosophy and morality of its time; but a new poetry, which is always contracting its limits, has grown up under the shadow of the old. Rossetti began it, but was too much of a painter in his poetry to follow it with a perfect devotion; and it became a movement when Mr. Lang and Mr. Gosse and Mr. Dobson devoted themselves to the most condensed of lyric poems, and when Mr. Bridges, a more considerable poet, elaborated a rhythm too delicate for any but an almost bodiless emotion, and repeated over and over the most ancient notes of poetry, and none but these. The poets who followed have either, like Mr. Kipling, turned from serious poetry altogether, and so passed out of the processional order, or speak out of some personal or spiritual passion in words and types and metaphors that draw one's imagination as far as possible from the complexities of modern life and thought. The change has been more marked in English painting, which, when intense enough to belong to the procession order, began to cast out things, as they are seen by minds plunged in the labour of life, so much before French painting that ideal art is sometimes called English art upon the Continent.

I see, indeed, in the arts of every country those faint lights and faint colours and faint outlines and faint energies which many call 'the decadence,' and which I, because I believe that the arts lie dreaming of things to come, prefer to call the autumn of the body. An Irish poet whose rhythms are like the cry of a sea-bird in autumn twilight has told its meaning in the line, 'The very sunlight's weary, and it's time to quit the plough.' Its importance is the greater because it comes to us at the moment when we are beginning to be interested in many things which positive science, the interpreter of exterior law, has always denied: communion of mind with mind in thought and without words, foreknowledge in dreams and in visions, and the coming among us of the dead, and of much else. We are, it may be, at a crowning crisis of the world, at the moment when man is about to ascend, with the wealth, he has been so long gathering, upon his shoulders, the stairway he has been descending from the first days. The first poets, if one may find their images in the *Kalevala*, had not Homer's preoccupation with things, and he was not so full of their excitement as Virgil. Dante added to poetry a dialectic which, although he made it serve his laborious ecstasy, was the invention of minds trained by the labour of life, by a traffic among many things, and not a spontaneous expression of an interior life; while Shakespeare shattered the symmetry of verse and of drama that he might fill them with things and their accidental relations to one another.

Each of these writers had come further down the stairway than those who had lived before him, but it was only with the modern poets, with Goethe and Wordsworth and Browning, that poetry gave up the right to consider all things in the world as a dictionary of types and symbols and began to call itself a critic of life and an interpreter of things as they are. Painting, music, science, politics, and even religion, because they have felt a growing belief that we know nothing but the fading and flowering of the world, have changed in numberless elaborate ways. Man has wooed and won the world, and has fallen weary, and not, I think, for a time, but with a weariness that will not end until the last autumn, when the stars shall be blown away like withered leaves. He grew weary when he said, 'These things that I touch and see and hear are alone real,' for he saw them without illusion at last, and found them but air and dust and moisture. And now he must be philosophical above everything, even about the arts, for he can only return the way he came, and so escape from weariness, by philosophy. The arts are, I believe, about to take upon their shoulders the burdens that have fallen from the shoulders of priests, and to lead us back upon our journey by filling our thoughts with the essences of things, and not with things. We are about to substitute once more the distillation of alchemy for the analyses of chemistry and for some other sciences; and certain of us are looking everywhere for the perfect alembic that no silver or golden drop may escape. Mr. Symons has written lately on M. Mallarmé's method, and has quoted him as saying that we should 'abolish the pretension, æsthetically an error, despite its dominion over almost all the masterpieces, to enclose within the subtle pages other than—for example—the horror of the forest or the silent thunder in the leaves, not the intense dense wood of the trees,' and as desiring to substitute for the old lyric afflatus or the enthusiastic personal direction of the phrase' words 'that take light from mutual reflection, like an actual trail of fire over precious stones,' and 'to make an entire word hitherto unknown to the language' 'out of many vocables.'

Mr. Symons understands these and other sentences to mean that poetry will henceforth be a poetry of essences, separated one from another in little and intense poems. I think there will be much poetry of this kind, because of an ever more arduous search for an almost disembodied ecstasy, but I think we will not cease to write long poems, but rather that we will write them more and more as our new belief makes the world plastic under our hands again. I think that we will learn again how to describe at great length an old man wandering among enchanted islands, his return home at last, his slow-gathering vengeance, a flitting shape of a goddess, and a flight of arrows, and yet to make all of these so different things 'take light by mutual reflection, like an actual trail of fire over precious stones,' and become 'an entire word,' the signature or symbol of a mood of the divine imagination as imponderable as 'the horror of the forest or the silent thunder in the leaves.'

1898

THE MOODS

Literature differs from explanatory and scientific writing in being wrought about a mood, or a community of moods, as the body is wrought about an invisible soul; and if it uses argument, theory, erudition, observation, and seems to grow hot in assertion or denial, it does so merely to make us partakers at the banquet of the moods. It seems to me that these moods are the labourers and messengers of the Ruler of All, the gods of ancient days still dwelling on their secret Olympus, the angels of more modern days ascending and descending upon their shining ladder; and that argument, theory, erudition, observation, are merely what Blake called 'little devils who fight for themselves,' illusions of our visible passing life, who must be made serve the moods, or we have no part in eternity. Everything that can be seen, touched, measured, explained, understood, argued over, is to the imaginative artist nothing more than a means, for he belongs to the invisible life, and delivers its ever new and ever ancient revelation. We hear much of his need for the restraints of reason, but the only restraint he can obey is the mysterious instinct that has made him an artist, and that teaches him to discover immortal moods in mortal desires, an undecaying hope in our trivial ambitions, a divine love in sexual passion.

1895

THE BODY OF THE
FATHER CHRISTIAN ROSENCRUX

The followers of the Father Christian Rosencrux, says the old tradition, wrapped his imperishable body in noble raiment and laid it under the house of their order, in a tomb containing the symbols of all things in heaven and earth, and in the waters under the earth, and set about him inextinguishable magical lamps, which burnt on generation after generation, until other students of the order came upon the tomb by chance. It seems to me that the imagination has had no very different history during the last two hundred years, but has been laid in a great tomb of criticism, and had set over it inextinguishable magical lamps of wisdom and romance, and has been altogether so nobly housed and apparelled that we have forgotten that its wizard lips are closed, or but opened for the complaining of some melancholy and ghostly voice. The ancients and the Elizabethans abandoned themselves to imagination as a woman abandons herself to love, and created great beings who made the people of this world seem but shadows, and great passions which made our loves and hatreds appear but ephemeral and trivial phantasies; but now it is not the great persons, or the great passions we imagine, which absorb us, for the persons and passions in our poems are mainly reflections our mirror has caught from older poems or from the life about us, but the wise comments we make upon them, the criticism of life we wring from their fortunes. Arthur and his Court are nothing, but the many-coloured lights that play about them are as beautiful as the lights from cathedral windows; Pompilia and Guido are but little, while the ever-recurring meditations and expositions which climax in the mouth of the Pope are among the wisest of the Christian age. I cannot get it out of my mind that this age of criticism is about to pass, and an age of imagination, of emotion, of moods, of revelation, about to come in its place; for certainly belief in a supersensual world is at hand again; and when the notion that we are 'phantoms of the earth and water' has gone down the wind, we will trust our own being and all it desires to invent; and when the external world is no more the standard of reality, we will learn again that the great Passions are angels of God, and that to embody them 'uncurbed in their eternal glory,' even in their labour for the ending of man's peace and prosperity, is more than to comment, however wisely, upon the tendencies of our time, or to express the socialistic, or humanitarian, or other forces of our time, or even 'to sum up' our time, as the phrase is; for Art is a revelation, and not a criticism, and the life of the artist is in the old saying, 'The wind bloweth where it listeth, and thou hearest the sound thereof, but canst not tell whence it cometh and whither it goeth; so is every one that is born of the spirit.'

1895

The Return of Ulysses

I

M. Maeterlinck, in his beautiful *Treasure of the Humble*, compares the dramas of our stage to the paintings of an obsolete taste; and the dramas of the stage for which he hopes, to the paintings of a taste that cannot become obsolete. 'The true artist,' he says, 'no longer chooses Marius triumphing over the Cimbrians, or the assassination of the Duke of Guise, as fit subjects for his art; for he is well aware that the psychology of victory or murder is but elementary and exceptional, and that the solemn voice of men and things, the voice that issues forth so timidly and hesitatingly, cannot be heard amidst the idle uproar of acts of violence. And therefore will he place on his canvas a house lost in the heart of the country, a door open at the end of a passage, a face or hands at rest.' I do not understand him to mean that our dramas should have no victories or murders, for he quotes for our example plays that have both, but only that their victories and murders shall not be to excite our nerves, but to illustrate the reveries of a wisdom which shall be as much a part of the daily life of the wise as a face or hands at rest. And certainly the greater plays of the past ages have been built after such a fashion. If this fashion is about to become our fashion also, and there are signs that it is, plays like some of Mr. Robert Bridges will come out of that obscurity into which all poetry, that is not lyrical poetry, has fallen, and even popular criticism will begin to know something about them. Some day the few among us, who care for poetry more than any temporal thing, and who believe that its delights cannot be perfect when we read it alone in our rooms and long for one to share its delights, but that they might be perfect in the theatre, when we share them friend with friend, lover with beloved, will persuade a few idealists to seek out the lost art of speaking, and seek out ourselves the lost art, that is perhaps nearest of all arts to eternity, the subtle art of listening. When that day comes we will talk much of Mr. Bridges; for did he not write scrupulous, passionate poetry to be sung and to be spoken, when there were few to sing and as yet none to speak? There is one play especially, *The Return of Ulysses*, which we will praise for perfect after its kind, the kind of our new drama of wisdom, for it moulds into dramatic shape, and with as much as possible of literal translation, those closing books of the

Odyssey which are perhaps the most perfect poetry of the world, and compels that great tide of song to flow through delicate dramatic verse, with little abatement of its own leaping and clamorous speed. As I read, the gathering passion overwhelms me, as it did when Homer himself was the singer, and when I read at last the lines in which the maid describes to Penelope the battle with the suitors, at which she looks through the open door, I tremble with excitement.

'PENELOPE: Alas! what cries! Say, is the prince still safe?
THE MAID: He shieldeth himself well, and striketh surely;
    His foes fall down before him. Ah! now what can I see?
    Who cometh? Lo! a dazzling helm, a spear
    Of silver or electron; sharp and swift
    The piercings. How they fall! Ha! shields are raised
    In vain. I am blinded, or the beggar-man
    Hath waxed in strength. He is changed, he is young. O strange!
    He is all in golden armour. These are gods
    That slay the suitors. (*Runs to Penelope.*) O lady, forgive me.
    Tis Ares' self. I saw his crispèd beard;
    I saw beneath his helm his curlèd locks.'

The coming of Athene helmed 'in silver or electron' and her transformation of Ulysses are not, as the way is with the only modern dramas that popular criticism holds to be dramatic, the climax of an excitement of the nerves, but of that unearthly excitement which has wisdom for fruit, and is of like kind with the ecstasy of the seers, an altar flame, unshaken by the winds of the world, and burning every moment with whiter and purer brilliance.

Mr. Bridges has written it in what is practically the classical manner, as he has done in *Achilles in Scyros*—a placid and charming setting for many placid and charming lyrics—

> *'And ever we keep a feast of delight*
> *The betrothal of hearts, when spirits unite,*
> *Creating an offspring of joy, a treasure*
> *Unknown to the bad, for whom*
> *The gods foredoom*
> *The glitter of pleasure*
> *And a dark tomb.'*

The poet who writes best in the Shakespearian manner is a poet with a circumstantial and instinctive mind, who delights to speak with strange voices and to see his mind in the mirror of Nature; while Mr. Bridges, like most of us to-day, has a lyrical and meditative mind, and delights to speak with his own voice and to see Nature in the mirror of his mind. In reading his plays in a Shakespearian manner, I find that he is constantly arranging his story in such and such a way because he has read that the persons he is writing of did such and such things, and not because his soul has passed into the soul of their world and understood its unchangeable destinies. His *Return of Ulysses* is admirable in beauty, because its classical gravity of speech, which does not, like Shakespeare's verse, desire the vivacity of common life, purifies and subdues all passion into lyrical and meditative ecstasies, and because the unity of place and time in the late acts compels a logical rather than instinctive procession of incidents; and if the Shakespearian *Nero: Second Part* approaches it in beauty and in dramatic power, it is because it eddies about Nero and Seneca, who had both, to a great extent, lyrical and meditative minds. Had Mr. Bridges been a true Shakespearian, the pomp and glory of the world would have drowned that subtle voice that speaks amid our heterogeneous lives of a life lived in obedience to a lonely and distinguished ideal.

II

THE MORE A POET RIDS his verses of heterogeneous knowledge and irrelevant analysis, and purifies his mind with elaborate art, the more does the little ritual of his verse resemble the great ritual of Nature, and become mysterious and inscrutable. He becomes, as all the great mystics have believed, a vessel of the creative power of God; and whether he be a great poet or a small poet, we can praise the poems, which but seem to be his, with the extremity of praise that we give this great ritual which is but copied from the same eternal model. There is poetry that is like the white light of noon, and poetry that has the heaviness of woods, and poetry that has the golden light of dawn or of sunset; and I find in the poetry of Mr. Bridges in the plays, but still more in the lyrics, the pale colours, the delicate silence, the low murmurs of cloudy country days, when the plough is in the earth, and the clouds darkening towards sunset; and had I the great gift of praising, I would praise it as I would praise these things.

1896

IRELAND AND THE ARTS

The arts have failed; fewer people are interested in them every generation. The mere business of living, of making money, of amusing oneself, occupies people more and more, and makes them less and less capable of the difficult art of appreciation. When they buy a picture it generally shows a long-current idea, or some conventional form that can be admired in that lax mood one admires a fine carriage in or fine horses in; and when they buy a book it is so much in the manner of the picture that it is forgotten, when its moment is over, as a glass of wine is forgotten. We who care deeply about the arts find ourselves the priesthood of an almost forgotten faith, and we must, I think, if we would win the people again, take upon ourselves the method and the fervour of a priesthood. We must be half humble and half proud. We see the perfect more than others, it may be, but we must find the passions among the people. We must baptize as well as preach.

The makers of religions have established their ceremonies, their form of art, upon fear of death, on the hope of the father in his child, upon the love of man and woman. They have even gathered into their ceremonies the ceremonies of more ancient faiths, for fear a grain of the dust turned into crystal in some past fire, a passion that had mingled with the religious idea, might perish if the ancient ceremony perished. They have renamed wells and images and given new meanings to ceremonies of spring and midsummer and harvest. In very early days the arts were so possessed by this method that they were almost inseparable from religion, going side by side with it into all life. But, to-day, they have grown, as I think, too proud, too anxious to live alone with the perfect, and so one sees them, as I think, like charioteers standing by deserted chariots and holding broken reins in their hands, or seeking to go upon their way drawn by the one passion which alone remains to them out of the passions of the world. We should not blame them, but rather a mysterious tendency in things which will have its end some day. In England, men like William Morris, seeing about them passions so long separated from the perfect that it seemed as if they could not be changed until society had been changed, tried to unite the arts once more to life by uniting them to use. They advised painters to paint fewer pictures upon canvas, and to burn more of them on plates; and they tried to persuade sculptors that a candlestick might be as beautiful as

WILLIAM BUTLER YEATS

a statue. But here in Ireland, when the arts have grown humble, they will find two passions ready to their hands, love of the Unseen Life and love of country. I would have a devout writer or painter often content himself with subjects taken from his religious beliefs; and if his religious beliefs are those of the majority, he may at last move hearts in every cottage. While even if his religious beliefs are those of some minority, he will have a better welcome than if he wrote of the rape of Persephone, or painted the burning of Shelley's body. He will have founded his work on a passion which will bring him to many besides those who have been trained to care for beautiful things by a special education. If he is a painter or a sculptor he will find churches awaiting his hand everywhere, and if he follows the masters of his craft our other passion will come into his work also, for he will show his Holy Family winding among hills like those of Ireland, and his Bearer of the Cross among faces copied from the faces of his own town. Our art teachers should urge their pupils into this work, for I can remember, when I was myself a Dublin art student, how I used to despond, when eagerness burned low, as it always must now and then, at seeing no market at all.

But I would rather speak to those who, while moved in other things than the arts by love of country, are beginning to write, as I was some sixteen years ago, without any decided impulse to one thing more than another, and especially to those who are convinced, as I was convinced, that art is tribeless, nationless, a blossom gathered in No Man's Land. The Greeks, the only perfect artists of the world, looked within their own borders, and we, like them, have a history fuller than any modern history of imaginative events; and legends which surpass, as I think, all legends but theirs in wild beauty, and in our land, as in theirs, there is no river or mountain that is not associated in the memory with some event or legend; while political reasons have made love of country, as I think, even greater among us than among them. I would have our writers and craftsmen of many kinds master this history and these legends, and fix upon their memory the appearance of mountains and rivers and make it all visible again in their arts, so that Irishmen, even though they had gone thousands of miles away, would still be in their own country. Whether they chose for the subject the carrying off of the Brown Bull, or the coming of Patrick, or the political struggle of later times, the other world comes so much into it all that their love of it would move in their hands also, and as much, it may be, as in the hands of the Greek craftsmen. In other words, I would have Ireland recreate the ancient arts, the arts as they were understood in Judæa, in India, in Scandinavia, in Greece and Rome, in every ancient land; as they were understood when they moved a whole people and not a few people who have grown up in a leisured class and made this understanding their business.

I think that my reader will have agreed with most that I have said up till now, for we all hope for arts like these. I think indeed I first learned to hope for them myself in Young Ireland Societies, or in reading the essays of Davis. An Englishman, with his belief in progress, with his instinctive preference for the cosmopolitan literature of the last century, may think arts like these parochial, but they are the arts we have begun the making of.

I will not, however, have all my readers with me when I say that no writer, no artist, even though he choose Brian Boroihme or S. Patrick for his subject, should try to make his work popular. Once he has chosen a subject he must think of nothing but giving it such an expression as will please himself. As Walt Whitman has written—

'The oration is to the orator, the acting is to the actor and actress,
not to the audience:
And no man understands any greatness or goodness but his own or the
indication of his own.'

He must make his work a part of his own journey towards beauty and truth. He must picture saint or hero, or hillside, as he sees them, not as he is expected to see them, and he must comfort himself, when others cry out against what he has seen, by remembering that no two men are alike, and that there is no 'excellent beauty without strangeness.' In this matter he must be without humility. He may, indeed, doubt the reality of his vision if men do not quarrel with him as they did with the Apostles, for there is only one perfection and only one search for perfection, and it sometimes has the form of the religious life and sometimes of the artistic life; and I do not think these lives differ in their wages, for 'The end of art is peace,' and out of the one as out of the other comes the cry: *Sero te amavi, Pulchritudo tam antiqua et tam nova! Sero te amavi!*

The Catholic Church is not the less the Church of the people because the Mass is spoken in Latin, and art is not less the art of the people because it does not always speak in the language they are used to.

I once heard my friend Mr. Ellis say, speaking at a celebration in honour of a writer whose fame had not come till long after his death, 'It is not the business of a poet to make himself understood, but it is the business of the people to understand him. That they are at last compelled to do so is the proof of his authority.' And certainly if you take from art its martyrdom, you will take from it its glory. It might still reflect the passing modes of mankind, but it would cease to reflect the face of God.

If our craftsmen were to choose their subjects under what we may call, if we understand faith to mean that belief in a spiritual life which is not confined to one Church, the persuasion of their faith and their country, they would soon discover that although their choice seemed arbitrary at first, it had obeyed what was deepest in them. I could not now write of any other country but Ireland, for my style has been shaped by the subjects I have worked on, but there was a time when my imagination seemed unwilling, when I found myself writing of some Irish event in words that would have better fitted some Italian or Eastern event, for my style had been shaped in that general stream of European literature which has come from so many watersheds, and it was slowly, very slowly, that I made a new style. It was years before I could rid myself of Shelley's Italian light, but now I think my style is myself. I might have found more of Ireland if I had written in Irish, but I have found a little, and I have found all myself. I am persuaded that if the Irishmen who are painting conventional pictures or writing conventional books on alien subjects, which have been worn away like pebbles on the shore, would do the same, they, too, might find themselves. Even the landscape-painter, who paints a place that he loves, and that no other man has painted, soon discovers that no style learned in the studios is wholly fitted to his purpose. And I cannot but believe that if our painters of Highland cattle and moss-covered barns were to care enough for their country to care for what makes it different from other countries, they would discover, when struggling, it may be, to paint the exact grey of the bare Burren Hills, and of a sudden it may be, a new style, their very selves. And I admit, though in this I am moved by some touch of fanaticism, that even when I see an old subject written of or painted in a new way, I am yet jealous for Cuchulain, and for Baile, and Aillinn, and for those grey mountains that still are lacking their celebration. I sometimes reproach myself because I cannot admire Mr. Hughes' beautiful, piteous *Orpheus and Eurydice* with an unquestioning mind. I say with my lips, 'The Spirit made it, for it is beautiful, and the Spirit bloweth where it listeth,' but I say in my heart, 'Aengus and Etain would have served his turn;' but one cannot, perhaps, love or believe at all if one does not love or believe a little too much.

And I do not think with unbroken pleasure of our scholars who write about German writers or about periods of Greek history. I always remember that they could give us a number of little books which would tell, each book for some one country, or some one parish, the verses, or the stories, or the events that would make every lake or mountain a man can see from his own door an excitement in his imagination. I would have some of them leave that work of theirs which will never lack hands, and begin to dig in Ireland, the garden of the future, understanding that here in Ireland the spirit of man may be about to wed the soil of the world.

Art and scholarship like these I have described would give Ireland more than they received from her, for they would make love of the unseen more unshakable, more ready to plunge deep into the abyss, and they would make love of country more fruitful in the mind, more a part of daily life. One would know an Irishman into whose life they had come—and in a few generations they would come into the life of all, rich and poor—by something that set him apart among men. He himself would understand that more was expected of him than of others because he had greater possessions. The Irish race would have become a chosen race, one of the pillars that uphold the world.

1901

The Galway Plains

L ady Gregory has just given me her beautiful *Poets and Dreamers*, and it has brought to mind a day two or three years ago when I stood on the side of Slieve Echtge, looking out over Galway. The Burren Hills were to my left, and though I forget whether I could see the cairn over Bald Conan of the Fianna, I could certainly see many places there that are in poems and stories. In front of me, over many miles of level Galway plains, I saw a low blue hill flooded with evening light. I asked a countryman who was with me what hill that was, and he told me it was Cruachmaa of the Sidhe. I had often heard of Cruachmaa of the Sidhe even as far north as Sligo, for the country people have told me a great many stories of the great host of the Sidhe who live there, still fighting and holding festivals.

I asked the old countryman about it, and he told me of strange women who had come from it, and who would come into a house having the appearance of countrywomen, but would know all that had happened in that house; and how they would always pay back with increase, though not by their own hands, whatever was given to them. And he had heard, too, of people who had been carried away into the hill, and how one man went to look for his wife there, and dug into the hill and all but got his wife again, but at the very moment she was coming out to him, the pick he was digging with struck her upon the head and killed her. I asked him if he had himself seen any of its enchantments, and he said, 'Sometimes when I look over to the hill, I see a mist lying on the top of it, that goes away after a while.'

A great part of the poems and stories in Lady Gregory's book were made or gathered between Burren and Cruachmaa. It was here that Raftery, the wandering country poet of ninety years ago, praised and blamed, chanting fine verses, and playing badly on his fiddle. It is here the ballads of meeting and parting have been sung, and some whose lamentations for defeat are still remembered may have passed through this plain flying from the battle of Aughrim.

'I will go up on the mountain alone; and I will come hither from it again. It is there I saw the camp of the Gael, the poor troop thinned, not keeping with one another; Och Ochone!' And here, if one can believe many devout people whose stories are in the book, Christ has walked upon the roads, bringing the needy to some warm fireside, and sending one of His Saints to anoint the dying.

I do not think these country imaginations have changed much for centuries, for they are still busy with those two themes of the ancient Irish poets, the sternness of battle and the sadness of parting and death. The emotion that in other countries has made many love songs has here been given, in a long wooing, to danger, that ghostly bride. It is not a difference in the substance of things that the lamentations that were sung after battles are now sung for men who have died upon the gallows.

The emotion has become not less, but more noble, by the change, for the man who goes to his death with the thought—

> *'It is with the people I was,*
> *It is not with the law I was,'*

has behind him generations of poetry and poetical life.

The poets of to-day speak with the voice of the unknown priest who wrote, some two hundred years ago, that *Sorrowful Lament for Ireland*, Lady Gregory has put into passionate and rhythmical prose—

> *'I do not know of anything under the sky*
> *That is friendly or favourable to the Gael,*
> *But only the sea that our need brings us to,*
> *Or the wind that blows to the harbour*
> *The ship that is bearing us away from Ireland;*
> *And there is reason that these are reconciled with us,*
> *For we increase the sea with our tears,*
> *And the wandering wind with our sighs.'*

There is still in truth upon these great level plains a people, a community bound together by imaginative possessions, by stories and poems which have grown out of its own life, and by a past of great passions which can still waken the heart to imaginative action. One could still, if one had the genius, and had been born to Irish, write for these people plays and poems like those of Greece. Does not the greatest poetry always require a people to listen to it? England or any other country which takes its tune from the great cities and gets its taste from schools and not from old custom, may have a mob, but it cannot have a people. In England there are a few groups of men and women who have good taste, whether in cookery or in books; and the great multitudes but copy them or their copiers. The poet must always prefer the community where the perfected minds express the people, to a community that is vainly seeking to copy the perfected minds. To have even perfectly the thoughts that can be weighed, the knowledge that can be got from books, the precision that can be learned at school, to belong to any aristocracy, is to be a little pool that will soon dry up. A people alone are a great river; and that is why I am persuaded that where a people has died, a nation is about to die.

1903

EMOTION OF MULTITUDE

I have been thinking a good deal about plays lately, and I have been wondering why I dislike the clear and logical construction which seems necessary if one is to succeed on the Modern Stage. It came into my head the other day that this construction, which all the world has learnt from France, has everything of high literature except the emotion of multitude. The Greek drama has got the emotion of multitude from its chorus, which called up famous sorrows, long-leaguered Troy, much-enduring Odysseus, and all the gods and heroes to witness, as it were, some well-ordered fable, some action separated but for this from all but itself. The French play delights in the well-ordered fable, but by leaving out the chorus it has created an art where poetry and imagination, always the children of far-off multitudinous things, must of necessity grow less important than the mere will. This is why, I said to myself, French dramatic poetry is so often a little rhetorical, for rhetoric is the will trying to do the work of the imagination. The Shakespearean Drama gets the emotion of multitude out of the sub-plot which copies the main plot, much as a shadow upon the wall copies one's body in the firelight. We think of King Lear less as the history of one man and his sorrows than as the history of a whole evil time. Lear's shadow is in Gloster, who also has ungrateful children, and the mind goes on imagining other shadows, shadow beyond shadow till it has pictured the world. In *Hamlet*, one hardly notices, so subtly is the web woven, that the murder of Hamlet's father and the sorrow of Hamlet are shadowed in the lives of Fortinbras and Ophelia and Laertes, whose fathers, too, have been killed. It is so in all the plays, or in all but all, and very commonly the sub-plot is the main plot working itself out in more ordinary men and women, and so doubly calling up before us the image of multitude. Ibsen and Maeterlinck have on the other hand created a new form, for they get multitude from the Wild Duck in the Attic, or from the Crown at the bottom of the Fountain, vague symbols that set the mind wandering from idea to idea, emotion to emotion. Indeed all the great Masters have understood, that there cannot be great art without the little limited life of the fable, which is always the better the simpler it is, and the rich, far-wandering, many-imaged life of the half-seen world beyond it. There are some who understand that the simple unmysterious things living as in a clear noon-light are of the nature of the sun, and that vague many-imaged things have in them the strength of the moon. Did not the Egyptian carve it on emerald that all living things have the sun for father and the moon for mother, and has it not been said that a man of genius takes the most after his mother?

1903

A Note About the Author

W.B. Yeats (1865–1939) was an Irish poet. Born in Sandymount, Yeats was raised between Sligo, England, and Dublin by John Butler Yeats, a prominent painter, and Susan Mary Pollexfen, the daughter of a wealthy merchant family. He began writing poetry around the age of seventeen, influenced by the Romantics and the Pre-Raphaelite Brotherhood, but soon turned to Irish folklore and the mystical writings of William Blake for inspiration. As a young man he joined and founded several occult societies, including the Dublin Hermetic Order and the Hermetic Order of the Golden Dawn, participating in séances and rituals as well as acting as a recruiter. While these interests continued throughout Yeats' life, the poet dedicated much of his middle years to the struggle for Irish independence. In 1904, alongside John Millington Synge, Florence Farr, the Fay brothers, and Annie Horniman, Yeats founded the Abbey Theatre in Dublin, which opened with his play *Cathleen ni Houlihan* and Lady Gregory's *Spreading the News* and remains Ireland's premier venue for the dramatic arts to this day. Although he was an Irish Nationalist, and despite his work toward establishing a distinctly Irish movement in the arts, Yeats—as is evident in his poem "Easter, 1916"—struggled to identify his idealism with the sectarian violence that emerged with the Easter Rising in 1916. Following the establishment of the Irish Free State in 1922, however, Yeats was appointed to the role of Senator and served two terms in the position. He was awarded the Nobel Prize in Literature in 1923, and continued to write and publish poetry, philosophical and occult writings, and plays until his death in 1939.

A Note from the Publisher

Spanning many genres, from non-fiction essays to literature classics to children's books and lyric poetry, Mint Edition books showcase the master works of our time in a modern new package. The text is freshly typeset, is clean and easy to read, and features a new note about the author in each volume. Many books also include exclusive new introductory material. Every book boasts a striking new cover, which makes it as appropriate for collecting as it is for gift giving. Mint Edition books are only printed when a reader orders them, so natural resources are not wasted. We're proud that our books are never manufactured in exce
quantity they need to be read and enjoyed.

bookfinity™

Discover more of your favorite classics with Bookfinity™.

- Track your reading with custom book lists.
- Get great book recommendations for your personalized Reader Type.
- Add reviews for your favorite books.
- AND MUCH MORE!

Visit **bookfinity.com** and take the fun Reader Type quiz to get started.

Enjoy our classic and modern companion pairings!

Classic & Modern

Printed in the USA
CPSIA information can be obtained
at www.ICGtesting.com
JSHW021957150824
68134JS00055B/2071